AUBURN
THE CLASSIC CITY

For My Children
John Clark Creager Smith
John Charles Thompson Smith
John Carl Patrick Smith

And My Grandchildren
Kathleen Ruth-Lucile Smith
Leah Evangeline Smith
Conner James Thompson Smith
Caleb Patrick Smith
Kendyl Jama Thompson Smith
Kaitlyn Thompson Jama Smith

John Martin Smith. Appointed by the Indiana Historical Society and Indiana Historical Bureau, John Martin Smith has served as DeKalb County historian since 1981.

THE MAKING OF AMERICA SERIES

AUBURN

THE CLASSIC CITY

JOHN MARTIN SMITH

ARCADIA PUBLISHING

ISBN 978-0-7385-2401-6

Published by Arcadia Publishing,
Charleston SC, Chicago IL, Portsmouth NH, San Francisco CA

Printed in the United States

Library of Congress control number: 2002109594

For all general information contact Arcadia Publishing at:
Telephone 843-853-2070
Fax 843-853-0044
E-Mail sales@arcadiapublishing.com
For customer service and orders:
Toll-Free 1-888-313-2665
Visit us on the Internet at www.arcadiapublishing.com

FRONT COVER: *AUBURN CITY BAND,* C. *1910. The band is riding on a McIntyre truck in a parade. The sign says, "The Auburn Automobile Company—The Most for the Money—Auburn, Indiana USA."*

CONTENTS

Introduction and Acknowledgments

I summon to my aid the muse of local history—the traditions of our own home—the deeds of our native heroes.

~William Gilmore Simms (1851)

Temples fall, statues decay, mausoleums perish, elegant phrases declared are forgotten, but good books are immortal.

~William T. Vernon

Writing a history of one's hometown is an awesome responsibility. I am not a true native, however. I was born on August 17, 1939, at Dr. Bonnell Souder's Hospital in Auburn, but grew up in Butler, graduated from Indiana University, and then moved to Auburn in July 1965 to practice law in the office of Edgar W. Atkinson, who had begun the practice in 1909.

Until I came to reside in Auburn in 1965, my contacts were limited to an occasional Saturday shopping expedition with my parents, a movie at the Court Theatre, a nude swim at the YMCA, a basketball game with the Windmills v. the Red Devils, or a date with an Auburn girl. (Auburn girls seemed prettier and more sophisticated than the Butler girls with whom we had spent 12 years of school!)

These contacts and my sense of historical observation perhaps make me as qualified as anyone to write this book. Some would say that history should be written by a disinterested objective person. I am not that! Local history is my passion. I write from the heart. I strive to place the history of our town into the big picture of national history.

Former Speaker of the United States House of Representatives Eugene "Tip" O'Neil once said, "All politics are local." I say, "All history is local." The history of our state, of our nation, is the sum of its parts. It is important to know and record the histories of those "parts," the histories of the cities, towns, and countries that make up the whole.

It is hoped that the readers of this book, present and future, will feel the essence of our town, of our Auburn, over the 165 years of its existence. Counting

SWINEFORD HOUSE. Located at the southwest corner of Main and Ninth Streets, the Swineford House was Auburn's leading hotel. Horse-drawn hacks brought travelers from the depots at Auburn Junction and West Seventh Street to downtown Auburn. The W.H. Kiblinger Company buggy factory is in the right background.

generations at 20 years each, 8.25 generations have passed through our town. A child born at the time of publication of this book, in 2002, could look back to a great-great-great-great-grandparent!

It is much more difficult to write a short book than a long book. Arcadia Publishing limits books in the *Making of America* series to 160 pages containing between 45,000 and 55,000 words with the balance in photographs. Therefore, an author has to synthesize 165 years of history into a relatively short space. This book is divided into 12 eras sub-titled with several descriptive words and a relevant quote. The index is limited to no more than 180 entries.

I have attempted to be as objective as possible while providing the reader with the "feel" of life in Auburn in each era. I am partial to the "common person," but have included the community leaders. Great things have been done by many common people. Perhaps they did not realize it at the time, but the advantage of historical hindsight can give them the recognition they deserve.

There are Auburns in 22 states: Alabama, Arkansas, California, Georgia, Illinois, Indiana, Iowa, Kansas, Kentucky, Maine, Massachusetts, Michigan, Nebraska, New Hampshire, New Jersey, New York, North Carolina, Pennsylvania, Texas, Washington, West Virginia, and Wyoming.

There are also place names containing the word Auburn, as follows: Mount Auburn, Massachusetts; East Auburn, Maine; Lake Auburn, Maine; Auburn

BARON DEKALB. DeKalb was the German nobleman for whom DeKalb County was named. He assisted the Americans in the Revolutionary War and was mortally wounded at the Battle of Camden.

Hills, Michigan; New Auburn, Minnesota; Auburn Township, Ohio; Mount Auburn, Ohio; Lake Auburn, Pennsylvania; Mount Auburn, Wisconsin; and New Auburn, Wisconsin.

The most recent census data shows that the largest Auburn (Alabama) had a population of 42,987 and the smallest (West Virginia) a population of 103 in 2000, while our Auburn had a population of 12,074.

What makes our Auburn special and unique? It is special and unique because it is "our town." It is here that our descendants were born and our ancestors died. Many of them lay buried in the Evergreen, Woodlawn, or Roselawn Cemeteries. We have trudged around the square hundreds of times during the DeKalb County Free Fall Fair. Our birth certificates are on record at the courthouse. We remember where we started school, went to junior high, and to high school. We cheered for the Red Devils or the Barons when they won and lamented when they lost.

We hope our children and grandchildren will stay here. Our town reflects our way of life, our values, our goals, and aspirations. There are bigger towns with more amenities, but we like our town just the way it is!

As I started writing this book, I re-read *Our Town*, the play by Thornton Wilder published in 1938. It is a play wherein it is the stage manager's task to present the life and times of Grover's Corners, New Hampshire at the beginning of the twentieth century. The residents—who grow up, work, marry, beget the next generation, and die—are sweet-natured, non-ambitious, and ordinary. And such is Wilder's point: to strip American life to its mundane fundamentals and illustrate, with a folksiness that belies the play's rather brutally unsentimental evocation of death, that our mortality is what we share and that, realize it or not, our mortality is what makes our most ordinary moments precious. In telling of the proposed contents of the cornerstone of a new bank being built, the stage manager says:

> We're putting in a Bible . . . and the Constitution of the United States—and a copy of William Shakespeare's plays. What do you say, folks? What do you think?
>
> Y'know—Babylon once had two million people in it, and all we know about 'em is the names of the kings and some copies of wheat contracts . . . and contracts for the sale of slaves. Yet every night all those families sat down to supper, and the father came home from work, and the smoke went up the chimney, same as here. And even in Greece and Rome, all we know about the real life of the people is what we can piece together out of the joking poems and the comedies they wrote for the theatre back then.
>
> So I'm going to have a copy of this play put in the cornerstone and the people a thousand years from now'll know a few simple facts about us—more than the Treaty of Versailles and the Lindbergh flight.
>
> See what I mean?
>
> So—people a thousand years from now—this is the way we were at the beginning of the twentieth century—This is the way we were; in our growing up and in our marrying and in our living and in our dying.

It is my goal to record "This is the way we were." While I cover the basic facts of our geography, our government, our industry, our schools, and the infrastructure of our town, I also convey a sense of the personal family lives and values of our ancestors and of ourselves.

I hope this book will be of help to genealogists in filling in the blanks about family members who were born, married, lived, and died in Auburn. Life is more than significant dates!

I am indebted to many persons for assistance in the preparation of this book.

My son Thompson Smith provided me with the time and secretarial help to prepare the manuscript. My secretary of 33 years, Sharon Kay George, was of great assistance. Tricia Boyer entered the manuscript into the computer and assisted in other ways. Lastly, my wife Barbara Clark Smith edited the text and has greatly improved my writing.

John Martin Smith
July 2002 at Auburn, Indiana

1. In the Beginning God Created:

Geology, Geography, and Plats (to 1835)

In the beginning God created the heavens and earth.

~Genesis 1:1

No modern urban planner would have selected the site of Auburn, Indiana as a location for a town. The original plat consisted of an area 4,054 feet north and south and 758 feet east and west containing 70 acres located near the west bank of Cedar Creek.

The soil is unstable. The water table is only 10 to 12 feet below the surface. The creek flooded frequently and left a marshy, wet area in its backwater that was a haven for mosquitoes and other insects. Cedar Creek did provide a possible water-powered mill site and was considered navigable with canoes and pirogues to connect Auburn with Fort Wayne via the St. Joe River.

The only reason the site was selected was that the venerable land speculator and entrepreneur Wesley Park owned the land and was able to persuade a LaGrange County lawyer and member of the Indiana General Assembly to designate his "paper town" the county seat of the newly created County of DeKalb.

Geologically, Cedar Creek has existed in some form for nearly 13,000 years. In historic times, it rose at Indian Lake in Fairfield Township, meandered southeasterly to the Waterloo area, flowed southerly to Auburn, then southwesterly into Allen County, where it became a tributary of the St. Joseph River at Cedarville.

Cedar Creek was originally in the Eel River/Wabash River Watershed, according to research by Mike Walter. At some point during the geological eons a glacier probably caused its route to change in the Cedar Canyons area, thus connecting it with the St. Joe River, which is in the Great Lakes Watershed. It is one of the few natural streams in the world that has naturally changed watersheds.

There were several Native American villages along the DeKalb County portion of Cedar Creek. The village nearest Auburn was on the east side of Cedar Creek where it crosses the line between Jackson Township and the original Butler Township line. The Potawatami Indians called Cedar Creek *Mes-kwah-wah-se-pe.*

Indiana became a territory in 1800 and a state in 1816. Many counties were soon created in southern Indiana along the Ohio and Wabash Rivers. Allen County was formed in 1824. Settlement of DeKalb County was delayed by the Great Black Swamp in northeastern Ohio. The swamp made travel from the east very difficult. Because land was available in central Indiana and was more easily accessible, there was no incentive to settle in DeKalb County.

The Fort Wayne Land office opened in 1823. Indian titles of what is now DeKalb County were extinguished by the Treaty of Carey Mission in 1828.

The original plat of Auburn is dated January 12, 1838, and Wesley Park and John B. Howe are shown as proprietors. The plat was lost for many years and was returned to DeKalb County by Howe in 1877, then recorded at DeKalb County in Plat Record 2, page 107.

By a deed dated May 23, 1836, Park deeded about half of the platted lots to Howe. This deed is recorded at LaGrange County in Deed Record 3, page 500. Park reserved all water and mill privileges, including the right to dam Cedar Creek for such purposes. This suggests that Wesley Park intended to establish a mill on Cedar Creek or perhaps sell a mill site. It is curious that the Park-to-Howe deed is dated about 20 months prior to the date of the plat. This may be explained by the fact that there may have been a prior drawing. The deed refers to "Gum" Street, which does not exist on the original plat.

CEDAR CREEK AT NINTH STREET. This view looks north toward Seventh Street. Before it was dredged and channeled, Cedar Creek was much wider and shallower.

In the meantime, land west of the original plat of Auburn had been platted by John and Ruth Spencer into "Spencer's Western Addition." By a deed dated January 20, 1838, many of the lots were conveyed to DeKalb County, conditional on Auburn being named the county seat.

The original plat contains four vertical tiers of lots and 20 horizontal tiers of lots. The east to west streets are numbered 1st through 12th and the streets are named Union (now 13th), Church (14th), Joseph (15th), Green (16th), Defiance (17th), Williams (18th), and Mary's (19th).

Each block is divided into four lots. The numbering system begins in the southwest corner, goes north to lot 20, east to the next tier, then south to lot 40, continuing up and down to lot 308 in the southeast corner. The areas constituting the public square and graveyard are not numbered but designated as such.

The two tiers of lots on the east and west sides run vertically and all others run horizontally. All streets are 66 feet wide and most lots are 4 rods in breadth by 8.5 rods in length (a rod is equivalent to 5.5 yards, or 16.5 feet). The Public Square is 20 rods in length by 70 rods in breadth, and the graveyard is 17 rods in length by 8 rods in breadth.

Neither Wesley Park nor John B. Howe ever recorded how they selected the name "Auburn." It is likely, however, that the name originated from the Oliver Goldsmith poem *Deserted Village*, which begins: "Sweet Auburn: Loveliest Village of the plain . . ."

One virgin tree survived in the town for many years. It was known as the "Old Elm" and was located in the middle of 13th Street between Main and Jackson Streets. It was the subject of many postcards. It survived into the early 1930s. A descendant of this huge tree is nearby in the middle of the block surrounded by South Main, West 13th, West 14th, and South Jackson Streets. It is one of the few hearty elms that survived Dutch Elm disease, which destroyed most of the majestic old elm trees in Auburn and much of the rest of the United States early in the twentieth century. It presently measures 16 feet in circumference at a point 5 feet above ground level, with a diameter of 5.09 feet.

2. Mud, Notched Ears, and Night Soil: The Pioneer Period (1836–1855)

Our parents found society in nature and repose in solitude, health in exertion and happiness in virtuous occupation. They doubtless felt at times a glow of generous pride in marking out a hitherto untrodden path, making the first clearings and building the first civilized tenements in the domain of nature and founding for themselves and their posterity a lasting and notable [town].

~W.H. McIntosh, *Auburn Courier,* June 4, 1891, on life in Auburn in 1848

What is now northern Indiana was the wild, wild West of the United States in this era. Virgin forests of huge trees among impenetrable swamps was what the pioneers found when they arrived in Auburn. About all the location had to offer was cheap lots, plenty of timber, and the murky, seldom navigated water of Cedar Creek.

Wesley Park and John B. Howe had prepared a plat, on paper at least, and the Indiana General Assembly had designated the phantom town as the seat of government for the newly formed County of DeKalb.

Why would anyone want to settle here? There was no town, there were no streets, there was no square, there was no government.

Most immigrants had escaped the horrors of feudal society in Europe where, despite generations of yeomen work, they still had nothing. They were willing to make great sacrifices for a fresh start, for a chance to own their own land, for hope for their children and grandchildren, and especially for the chance to determine their own destiny in a free society, albeit under very difficult economic and environmental conditions.

Many of these pilgrims journeying to DeKalb County had indentured themselves in New York or elsewhere for their passage from Europe. Some had previously settled in Ohio or further east; however, as those areas filled with settlers or the value of land doubled from \$1.25 an acre to \$2.50 an acre, they were ready to move further west. Some were children of immigrants following the tradition of their parents to move west.

Sometimes groups came from specific areas such as Stark County, Ohio. Frequently one family came to DeKalb County from a particular area and thereafter encouraged relatives or friends to move here as well.

The first settler in Auburn was surely Wesley Park, who built a double-log house on Lot 161 in the original plat, which is presently designated as 304 North Cedar Street.

If DeKalb County and Auburn had a father, it would be Wesley Park. While John B. Howe was shown as the co-platter of Auburn, his only role was to grease the General Assembly's designation of Auburn as the county seat. If Park was father, his faithful wife Sophia was the town's mother.

Wesley Park was everything to the new county and town. He nurtured their social and economic growth. His log house was the tavern and seat of government. He served in several offices in county government. He was the land agent and a public-spirited and patriotic man.

Out of the 306 platted lots, he had promised to donate 102 to the county to be sold to finance the establishment of county government and a basic infrastructure. Byron Bunnel was appointed agent of DeKalb County to sell the county lots. Likewise, John Spencer had committed multiple lots in his Western Addition to the County of DeKalb.

WESLEY PARK HOUSE AT 311 SOUTH MAIN STREET. James Cosper built this brick house for Wesley Park in 1840. It served as the courthouse and treasurer's office for a short time until the courthouse building was finished.

The first court was held in Park's house in 1838 with Charles Ewing presiding. He was the brother to William and George Ewing of Fort Wayne, who were well known fur traders. Park wrote, "During the sitting of court, it had to suspend till dinner was cooked, this gave the judge time for a nap which was very desirable, as he was generally fatigued and sometimes rather boozy."

In this era, there was a president judge, who was a lawyer, and two associate judges. The first two associate judges were Jacob Walborn and Thomas L. Yates. They were not lawyers, but functioned like a two-man jury that could out-vote the president judge. This arrangement was apparently a reflection of the pioneers' disdain for kings and for government in general. Justice was retained in the hands of "the people" via the associate judges.

Yates was from the Spencerville area and appeared in court in a fox skin hunting hat and coarse shirt. Park, who was both sheriff and clerk at the time, reported that Yates was a good judge, but:

> one day he got drunk and sentenced one Joseph Bashford, to receive a whipping, and swore that as he was the court and had passed sentence he would inflict the penalty; as the judge was making toward the criminal with the avowed intention, I seized him, and giving him a whirl told him plainly that if the court persisted in inflicting the penalty threatened, the sheriff would put the court "up the ladder." Upon this, the court acknowledged the authority of the sheriff, and adjourned peaceably.

The upper chamber of Park's cabin served as the jail and prisoners had to climb a ladder to get there. The ladder was then removed—thus, the judge was to be jailed by being put "up the ladder."

One of the first orders of business was to build a real jail. The sale of lots by the county was to provide funds for county capital improvements and government expenses, but the lots sold slowly. Specifications for a jail prepared in 1838 provided:

> Said jail to consist of one ground room, sixteen feet square inside of the walls, The upper soil where the jail stands shall be removed and three sticks of timber one foot square and twenty feet long shall be bedded ten inches into the ground, twenty feet apart from the outside of the two extremes, upon which a floor shall be laid of timber a foot thick and eight to sixteen inches wide making a floor twenty feet square upon which said jail shall be built of double walls of each side two feet thick. The inside wall shall be eight feet high between floors. The jail was to have a shingle roof and be lighted with one four-light window of 8 x 10 glass. It was to be secured by iron grates of inch square bars running at right angles, three inches apart.

Lots 169 and 170 were reserved for the jail. These were the present sites of the Auburn City Hall at 210 South Cedar Street and the former county jail at 208

South Cedar Street. In 1846, the grand jury, which was charged with the annual inspection of the county jail then, as now, reported:

> Inspected county jail and find the same suitable for the safe keeping and accommodation of prisoners confined there in, provided the prisoners have no assistance from without, in which case, the said prison would prove a very poor barrier to gentlemen wishing egress.

A second jail was authorized in 1851 and finished in 1852. It was designed by architect B.G. Cosgrave and built by Jefferson Wallace for $1,000. It had living quarters for the sheriff on the upper floor. It was the scene of the escape of a trio of "rascals who posted two of their number at a barred window which faced the street to sing, talk, and otherwise distract the jailer while the third of them tunneled a passage under the floor which they used to escape later that night."

The Auburn Post Office was established March 5, 1839, with Wesley Park appointed as postmaster. He served until October 6, 1845, when Nelson Payne was appointed. Payne was succeeded by Alonzo Watkins on May 5, 1849; Egbert B. Mott on February 10, 1851; and Timothy R. Dickenson on June 15, 1863.

Meanwhile, the infant county's officials were making plans for a permanent courthouse. At the May 1840 session of the Commissioners' Court, Thomas J. Freeman, Wesley Park, and Nelson Payne were appointed superintendents for the construction of such a building. It was to be located on the Public Square with dimensions of:

> thirty feet north and south, and forty feet east and west, six feet of which shall be a portico, four feet to stairs and wood rooms, leaving courthouse thirty feet long. Two front doors and an alley from each to circle fronting the judge's bench which was to be elevated a few feet above the floor. The clerk's seat and table to be in front of the bench. The criminal's box also to be in front of the bench. The rooms to be lighted by eleven twenty-four light windows above and below. The front of the portico to be supported by four turned pillars fifteen inches in diameter.

Funds for the erection of the courthouse were to be obtained through the sale of lots belonging to the county other than those set aside for the financing of the jail and for other reasons.

At an 1841 Commissioners' Court session, the specific plans were received, approved, and bids were requested. Work was to begin by July 1, 1842. James Hite, a carpenter living southeast of Auburn, received the contract for the sum of $800. Lyman Chidsey assisted him in framing the building. The project apparently progressed slowly, as Judge Mott reported that when he first came to DeKalb County in 1843, the Public Square around the courthouse was partially logged, but burned off, and the frame of the courthouse was up, but not enclosed.

AUBURN AT MAIN AND SEVENTH, LOOKING WEST. This c. 1870 image is one of the earliest known photographs of Auburn. The street in the foreground is Main Street, and three churches are visible—Baptist at near right, Catholic at far right, and Methodist at center right. The fences surrounding houses and the board sidewalks are clearly shown.

The building was completed in the fall of 1843 and, on April 29, 1844, the first court session was held in the new structure.

The county's first permanent courthouse was most attractive from an architectural standpoint and must have been the pride of the citizenry. It undoubtedly made a substantial contribution to the development of the county during the next decade.

It soon became apparent, however, that the courthouse was inadequate in size to meet the needs of a fast growing county. In 1845, S.W. Sprott, who served as clerk and recorder from 1841 to 1851, was authorized to erect a building for his use on the southwest corner of the Public Square at a cost not to exceed $200, to which an additional $50 was later added. In the fall of 1846, a separate office building was constructed on the northwest corner of the Public Square for the use of the auditor. In 1847, John Morris was permitted to erect a private law office on the west side of the Public Square. Morris was limited to a structure 20 feet square, was to occupy it until such time as it was wanted for public use, and was to pay $1 annual rent.

Life in early Auburn was difficult. At first, all settlers lived in log cabins that were built from the large trees in the area. The raising of a cabin provided some degree of social activity. The whole town turned out to help. The women brought food for the workers and frequently worked on a quilt. There was a celebration

FIRST DEKALB COUNTY COURTHOUSE. This handsome building stood on the square from 1843 to 1864. The second courthouse replaced it in 1865.

when the cabin was finished. On one occasion, Wesley Park sponsored a foot race between women and awarded a lot to the victor.

Most cabins were 14 by 14 feet. Some had doors, others only a hide hung over the opening. Beds were swung from the walls. Most had crude chimneys made of sticks daubed with mud.

Several pioneer accounts of this era lamented the loneliness. There was not much to do other than work. Wolves howled all night. There was also a fear of the Native Americans who remained in the area. No reports have been found as to any harm done by Native Americans in Auburn or DeKalb County, but they were universally feared based on stories from other areas. The last Indians were physically removed from DeKalb County in 1842.

Food was available by hunting, gathering, and growing. Deer and pheasant were abundant. Small game was easy to get. Wild cranberries, raspberries, strawberries, and other berries were available in season. Many pioneers bought two lots, one for a home and the other for a garden plot. Some raised livestock. A cow provided milk and was then butchered for meat. Chickens provided eggs and then meat. Hogs were easy to raise and could generally forage for their own food.

All animals were at "open range." That is, they were not fenced in, but could roam through the town at will. The only fences were around the houses and the courthouse. Cattle and hogs were identified by notched ears, the patterns of which were registered with the clerk of the court. Cows wore bells that had distinctive tones. Children were often sent to "fetch the cows" at milking time. The closest mill in the early days was Wolcott's Mill, now Wollcottville, a distance of 25 miles from Auburn. In 1842, a mill was built on the St. Joe River at Orange and, in 1845, a mill was built on the St. Joe at Spencerville. This decreased the distance the settlers needed to travel to mill.

A sawmill was built in 1841 by Wesley Park and David Ogden on Cedar Creek in the northeast part of Auburn. It was later purchased by David Ogden and then Samuel Haines Sr. and Samuel Haines Jr. The sawmill was water powered, but could only operate during periods of high water when there was sufficient water to move the wheel. Sawmills of this era were called "muley mills" and consisted of a vertical blade which operated on an "up and down" basis. The circular saw was not in general use in this area until about 1870, when steam engines came into common use. The sawmill provided a supply of lumber that could be used to build more sophisticated "frame buildings" as compared to the primitive log structures.

The availability of lumber drew several carpenters, builders, and cabinet makers to Auburn. Two early cabinet makers were Inzonan and Sherlock. Resident carpenters included James Cosper, Lyman Chidsey, Riley Jacobs, David J. Shoemaker, and Samuel W. Russell.

In 1841, Abel Forshay and Asa Chappell established a brick kiln near the west edge of Auburn.

After Wesley Park's log house burned in December 1840, he engaged James Cosper to build the handsome brick house at 311 South Main Street (Lot 61). Park moved the office of county treasurer to his new home. The county commissioners and circuit and probate courts met in the house until the courthouse was completed in 1844.

Basic economic principles provide that where there is a demand, a supply will soon develop. While the population of Auburn in 1840 was only about 40 persons, merchants began to recognize that Auburn needed a supply of goods to be brought in and placed for sale.

Thomas J. Freeman sold groceries and spirituous liquors. O.A. Parsons with George Wright traded in foreign and domestic goods, jewelry, drugs, and medicines under the name O.A. Parsons and Company. Charles Stimely had a gunsmith shop on South Main Street (Lots 55 and 56) in 1843. Isaac Savage opened a gunsmith shop in 1847. In 1844, Philip Fluke built a tannery at the northwest corner of Seventh and Jackson Streets. This provided a means of tanning hides and pelts for leather and fur. Soon, Henry Moneysmith set up a blacksmith shop and William Albright opened a harness shop.

The population of Auburn nearly doubled from 1840 to 1841. In October of 1841, the entire town was sickly with the "fevers." James Cosper took a census of the town and found 72 inhabitants, of which only 2 were not sick. Cosper had brought a barrel of meat, a bag of coffee, and a 10-gallon churn filled with dried fruit from Ohio. These provisions were essential to the fledgling town.

Three doctors had recently arrived and were kept busy administering the standard prescription of calomel and quinine. These doctors were J. Ross, R.B.

Cooper, and Eli Pritchard. Soon the doctors themselves were afflicted. Some pioneers advocated the use of herbs and roots, but whiskey was considered one of the best remedies.

David Hart was a professed "coon hunter" who claimed he had "studied medicine" with a Native American and prescribed various Native American remedies for the prevailing diseases and disorders from his whiskey shop. His prescriptions were "Gratis and Given in friendship."

Auburn was generally a very unhealthy place during the wet seasons of the year. The land was low and wet swamps abounded. Mosquitoes and other insects were abundant. W.H. McIntosh stated that, in 1845:

> the dread ague chill visited alike villager and settler and the mill dam north of the village was deemed a breeder of fever of the same insidious potency of the interminable woods and oozy swamps outlying and the evening breezes of springtime mingled the odors to poison the else balmy air of the season.

The mill pond was the subject of a nuisance suit filed in the DeKalb Circuit Court in 1845. It was alleged that the mill pond was an unhealthy place that contributed to the illness of the residents. The right of the owner to maintain it was upheld, however.

In 1846, another outbreak of the ague and fever occurred with many relying on McLan's Liver Pills and McKenzie's Tonic Febrifuge for relief.

Roads were essential to the growth of any town and to Auburn in particular. Two pioneer roads intersected in Auburn. The Fort Wayne to Coldwater Road was a major north-south route. It is presently Coldwater Road in Fort Wayne, which goes north to the Allen–DeKalb County line and then angles northeasterly along the route of County Road 11A, intersecting County Road 427, and then into Auburn via Wayne Street (formerly known as Fort Wayne Road), Ensley Avenue, and then South Main Street. It generally followed Main Street through town, continued north on County Road 427 to Waterloo, then north on County Road 427 to Pleasant Lake, Angola, and Coldwater, where it intersected the Michigan Road. The major east-west road was the Goshen-Defiance Road which went from Goshen, Indiana to Defiance, Ohio. It is now the approximate location of State Road 8 through Auburn.

In 1838, the DeKalb County Commissioners appropriated $800 each for the improvement of the Fort Wayne to Coldwater and Goshen-Defiance Roads. Other roads were authorized by the DeKalb County Commissioners, and viewers and surveyors were appointed to locate and document them. These roads were just paths through the wilderness. They tended to follow the high ground to avoid swamps and low areas. They were muddy in the fall and spring, dusty in the summer, and a maze of frozen ruts in the winter. Streams were forded at appropriate places.

The first bridge over Cedar Creek was "near the southeast corner of the village plat," presumably on East 19th Street, which extended southeasterly to the

Spencerville area. East 19th Street (extended) was later known as "The Old Brick Road." The bridge was built by Wellman McGinnes, supervised by S.W. Ralston on behalf of the DeKalb County Commissioners.

There was no governmental mechanism for improving the streets in Auburn. In 1849, a petition was filed with the DeKalb County Commissioners, who approved the creation of town government for Auburn and set an election to be held September 22, 1849. Notices were posted at the post office maintained by Timothy R. Dickinson, the store of Nelson Payne, and the west door of the courthouse. Alenzo Watkins was elected chairman and John Morris clerk. The town was divided into five wards. The trustees elected were O.A. Parsons, First Ward; Wesley Park, Second Ward; Nelson Payne, Third Ward; Reverend James T. Bliss, Fourth Ward; and Joel E. Hendricks, Fifth Ward.

A total of 30 men voted at this first election: T.R. Dickinson, O.A. Parsons, Reverend James T. Bliss, E.B. Mott, F. Jones, A. Watkins, John Morris, Isaac Jones, William B. Dancer, William Albright, J.H. Ford, Daniel Stroh, Z. Tanner, Daniel Hartrough, S.W. Ralston, John Bolinger, George Wagoner, Stephen Latson, Phillip Fluke, C. Stimely, A. Plum, M. Waterman, W. Park, John Johnston, Lewis Weaver, Harrison Jones, E. Wetsel, E.R. Woodbury, Henry Curtis, and George Webb.

BRICK KILN. The brick kiln on the west edge of town produced bricks for early Auburn buildings. The horse-powered mill mixed clay with water; the clay was put into wooden, sun-dried molds; and the bricks were then fired in the kilns in the background.

The first meeting of the Board of Trustees of the Town of Auburn was held on September 26, 1849 at the office of the DeKalb County treasurer on the square. Joel E. Hendricks was elected president of the board, Timothy R. Dickenson was elected town clerk, Egbert B. Mott was elected treasurer, and William B. Dancer was elected town assessor. By-laws were adopted and a tax rate of 50¢ per $100 valuation was established. This tax could be "worked out" by physically working to maintain the streets at the rate of 75¢ per day under the supervision of the trustee of the taxpayer's ward.

The first general election was held May 6, 1850, with 43 votes cast. The town re-incorporated in 1852 under a new act passed by the Indiana General Assembly pursuant to the 1852 Indiana Constitution.

By 1850, some progress had been made in the growth of the town, but W. H. McIntosh reported, "Houses were scattered at wide intervals; logs lay upon the courthouse square and papaw bushes grew rank and tall."

John Butt is an example of an immigrant who arrived in Auburn in 1850. W.H. McIntosh described him:

> John Butt, long closely associated with those to whom the town's interests were entrusted, was an emigrant from England to this country and locality. He first essayed pioneer work upon a farm and in later years took pleasure in recounting his experience as a settler. To fell

ENSLEY HOUSE. Located at 1335 South Jackson Street and built by Amos Hutchins for George Ensley, this house is of classic Greek Revival architecture.

> a tree he hacked for a long time wearily, all around the height of the proposed stump. And by dint of patient labor, finally brought down the tree in triumph. But his specialty was not in tree-felling. About 1850, he became a resident of Auburn and kept a grocery store in a small frame which stood on the lot where now John Hebel has his fine residence. He became proprietor of the Weaver House which stood on the present site of the Swineford House, and from this stand, ran a daily line of hacks between Angola and Fort Wayne. Removing to Waterloo, he was long proprietor of a hotel there, which he traded for Auburn property, with Frank Ryan, ex-county treasurer, and once more and finally made his home at this place.

A handsome house at 1335 South Jackson Street was built by Amos Hutchins for George Ensley. Now known as the Ensley House, it is an example of the classic Greek Revival architecture of the 1850s.

Industry continued to develop gradually. John Parnell built an ashery for the manufacture of pearl-ash. John Tridell opened a small foundry. Phillip Grake brought a "daguerreotype apparatus" when he migrated from Stark County, Ohio, but soon sold it to a party "who failed in its prosperous use, and soon moved away, taking it along." Thus it is possible that photographs were taken in Auburn as early as 1849.

The Pioneer Hardware store was established in 1850 and continues at the same location today at 203 South Main Street as Auburn City Hardware under the ownership of Robert Kokenge.

The first circus in Auburn appeared in 1852 as a traveling show. John McCane had a basket factory and employed local boys and girls to strip bark off wood in preparation for making baskets.

In 1853, the Auburn Town Board authorized sidewalks to be built at a width of 10 feet and authorized the planting of shade trees. It is likely that many of the present fine shade trees of Auburn were planted at this time.

The 1852 Indiana Constitution made some profound changes in Indiana law. The Constitutional Convention started October 7, 1850 and adjourned February 10, 1851 after adopting a new constitution to be submitted to the people for a vote. The representative from DeKalb and Steuben Counties was Edward May of Angola, an outspoken advocate of African Americans' rights and suffrage. When the issue of "Negro suffrage" was put to a vote, May's was the lone vote in favor of giving blacks the right to vote.

There were no public schools in Auburn until after 1852. Prior to that time, there were several private or "select" schools. The first school recorded was a "Subscription School" taught by Miss Jane Bailey in 1840, which was held in a "deserted, partly unfinished building which was also used for meetings." Parents paid a daily or weekly fee for the children to attend.

In 1843, the Union Township trustee retained Messrs. Beck and McCrum of Richland Township to build a school west of the Steifel and Wolf Store.

This building was also used by the county for court purposes. The school was conducted in 1843 and 1844 by Egbert B. Mott, a lawyer who also served as president judge of the court.

In 1849 and 1850, Dr. Joel E. Hendricks conducted a school in the northeast room on the second story of the courthouse. He was later associated with James Colgrove in conducting the Newville Academy. It is said that he "gave theory and practice of mathematics to an extent and thoroughness never since equaled in the limits of this county."

Chester P. Hodge conducted an academy in the upper floor of the jail, which was attended by the children of the Walsworth, Altenberg, and Cosper families.

The 1852 law entrusted schools to the towns and townships and authorized a school tax to be levied for the financial support of public schools. On May 14, 1853, an election was held for the selection of school trustees and a vote as to a school tax. Of the 25 votes cast, 22 were in favor of the school tax.

The school trustees scheduled a meeting on August 9, 1853 to determine whether or not to build a schoolhouse; however, the taxpayers were indifferent and no meeting was held. The school trustees then rented a log cabin from O.C. Houghton for $2 and Messrs. Berry and Houghton were employed to adapt the building for school use and Jonathon Hall was contracted to supply eight cords of firewood for $1 per cord.

At a special meeting held November 29, 1853, the trustees determined to have two free schools in Auburn. John Dancer was hired at $60 for 66 days of school at the Number 1 (north) school, and Miss Abigail Wolsey was hired at $48 for 66 days of school at the Number 2 (south) school, each to supply his or her own room and board. There were 160 students when school started December 7, 1853. Parents could send their children to either school.

The settlers undoubtedly worshiped privately in their own way from the time they arrived in Auburn; however, the pioneer town was not without religious institutions.

It was not until 1844 that the Presbyterians and Methodists organized churches. The Fort Wayne Presbyterians sent Reverend James T. Bliss to Auburn in October 1844. The Bear Creek Church southeast of Auburn was organized at the same time. Reverend Bliss held services at both churches each Sunday.

The Methodist Church assigned Reverend Samuel Lamb to a charge including Auburn. The full charge was "ninety miles around" and, therefore, services could be held in Auburn "but once in four weeks."

Wesley Park, a devoted Methodist, was sensitive to the complaints of the Methodist parishioners that they had services only once a month as compared to the Presbyterians, who had services each Sabbath day. He therefore donated the east half of Lot 139 (154 East Seventh Street) for a church. Fortunately, Reverend Lamb was a carpenter in his secular life. He laid out the frame and supervised the construction from donated materials and with donated labor. Work proceeded so slowly that the church was not finished until 1850. Elder Robinson of Fort Wayne dedicated the building before a large crowd. People came from a 10-mile radius to

PRESBYTERIAN CHURCH. Built in 1851 at the southeast corner of West Twelfth and South Jackson Streets, this handsome building was moved west several blocks to the McKinney Harrison School grounds when the present church was built in 1876. The old church was used by the school for various purposes, including a wood shop.

large meetings. The first Sunday school convention was held in a grove in the south part of Auburn in 1850. This was a large event dominated by children's exercises, including a parade of wagons decorated with banners, and with children singing religious songs. Mary Mott's children, Sheridan and Grenville, recited Bible verses. A potluck dinner was held at noon, followed by more exercises and preaching.

Not to be outdone by the Methodists, the Presbyterians built a frame church that was completed in 1851. It was located at 601 South Jackson Street. The building was later moved to the McKinney-Harrison school grounds and was used for various purposes by the school.

The Baptists had churches in several locations in DeKalb County from the earliest settlement. On August 13, 1853, a group met at the courthouse to organize a Baptist church. At this meeting, W.W. Welker was moderator and S.B. Ward clerk. The purpose of the meeting, as presented by Joseph Wolsey, was an initiatory step towards the forming of a church in Auburn.

An organization was formed on September 15, 1853. Letters had been obtained in the meantime from the parent church and were presented by Joseph Wolsey, Jacob Hick, John Thomas, Isaac Kelley, G.R. Baker, Philo Sanford, Ann Thomas, Vesta M. Ward, Hanna Baker, Sarah Kelley, Eliza Draggoo, Harriet Sandford, S.B. and Laura Ward, John Thomas Jr., Sophia Lumford, Eliza Ashleman, and Sarah J. Housel, of Auburn. These parties constituted the original membership of the first

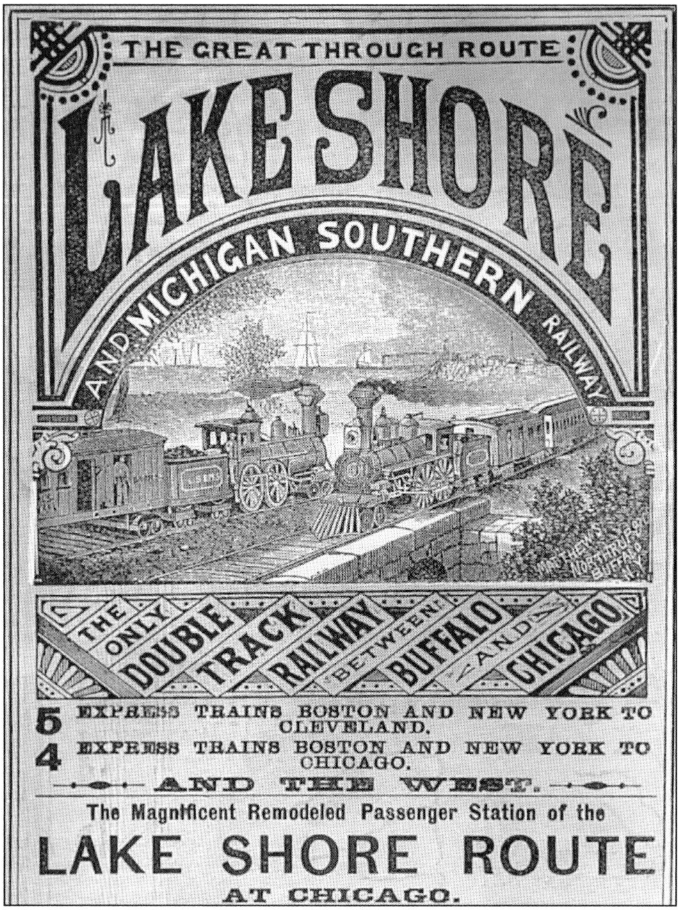

LAKESHORE & MICHIGAN SOUTHERN RAILWAY TIMETABLE. The Lakeshore went through Butler (then Jarvis), Waterloo, and Corunna in 1856, enabling those towns to grow and expand while Auburn was left isolated.

Baptist church in Auburn. At this meeting, G.R. Baker was appointed deacon and S.B. Ward was appointed clerk. Elder Ward became the first pastor. Elder A. Town was his successor for a short time, but he moved west, taking with him a large number of members. This resulted in the suspension of church work and finally to the disbanding of the church. Having no building of their own, the Baptist meetings had been held at the courthouse and at the Methodist and Presbyterian churches.

Then as now, liquor was the bane of the society. Taverns serving whiskey and beer were among the first businesses in the infant village. While not prohibited, liquors were heavily taxed by the county in the form of liquor licenses. Some persons could not resist the temptation of a hard drink and became hopeless alcoholics to the detriment of their wives and children, who often became public charges.

To combat the demon of booze, citizens organized the Sons of Temperance, Auburn Division Number 251. Meetings were held in the southeast room of the courthouse. Thus began a long effort to prohibit alcoholic beverages in Auburn.

While the town's growth had been steady, real growth would not be possible until better transportation was available. Cedar Creek was not navigable on a commercial basis. Auburn was about 25 miles from the Wabash and Erie Canal, and the roads were barely useable for much of the year. Auburn commerce was limited to a 5- to 10-mile radius. The only raw materials available were those found locally, such as timber to be sawn into lumber, woods that could be made into baskets, and grain raised locally. There was no market for agricultural products or for manufactured products other than in the immediate vicinity.

In 1851, the Auburn & Eel River Valley Railroad announced that a railroad would be built from Logansport to Auburn. The railroad changed its name to the Logansport & Northern Indiana Railroad by a resolution dated August 3, 1853, and projected its north terminus to Butler (then called Jarvis) to connect with the Lakeshore & Michigan Southern Railroad, already under construction at that time.

Surveyors placed stakes throughout the county to delineate the centerline of a 99-foot right-of-way. Buyers then started purchasing land from owners. The railroad was not built, however, until 1872 under the name of the Detroit, Eel River & Illinois Railroad, which had been organized on November 4, 1868. (This railroad will be referred to hereafter as the "Vandalia.")

In the meantime, the Lakeshore & Michigan Southern Railroad was built through Butler, Waterloo, Sedan, and Corunna.

Without a railroad, Auburn was to languish as a viable town and commercial center. W.H. McIntosh stated that, in 1855, "Auburn was 'in the depths' and it is not surprising that a part of her residents removed elsewhere and it is to the lasting credit of those who remained that they so stoutly stood by and joined their fortune with that of the town."

Lots were not selling well, with some going for as little as $30. Another was traded for a gold watch. Many lots "were mere swamp holes grown to rank vegetation, colonized by frogs and exerting from their stagnant surface miasmatic vapor which gave rise to chills and fever."

Crime was rampant. Northeastern Indiana had become a haven for criminals, who were attracted to the wild terrain and the lack of active law enforcement. W.K. Straight was elected sheriff of DeKalb County in 1850 and did his best to fight crime. W.H. McIntosh described him as a man of remarkable size, strength, and courage, his mere presence and personal appearance being often sufficient to calm the desperate men he sometimes had to handle:

> at one time when court was in session, it adjourned about four o'clock in the afternoon and Straight being a great hunter, at once took down his gun and started out into the woods that then covered the creek bottom close by. By dark, he got home with a nice deer, but was told a prisoner had escaped from the old log jail. He at once saddled a horse and without waiting for supper started off for the place of "Old Sile Doty" a noted character of those days. It was about eleven o'clock when he reached his destination and he pushed into the cabin without warning, and found eight men present, his prisoner being one of them. All arose

at once and showed fight. Straight coolly, but firmly told them he would not molest anyone but the man he came after and that one, he proposed to take. A brief talk convinced the men, that Straight was not to be trifled with. He took his man and brought him back, though he looked to see the other fellows dodge out from behind trees on the dark road to stop him.

At another time a horse thief was escaping going through Steuben and LaGrange counties, and Straight followed so close on his track that the fellow left his horse and plunged into a swamp. Straight followed and finally tired the man out. When found, he was lying in the thick brush, and could easily have killed the sheriff, who had passed within a few feet.

On another occasion he wanted a man over in Ohio, not far from Hicksville and on going over there, called on A.P. Edgerton and said, "I want a man who is hiding near here." "Well," said Edgerton, "go to the state line, just bend it east till it gets beyond the man you want, then take him and after you are gone, I'll hand the line back again for you." Straight got his man.

Thus we leave this era with Auburn "in the depths." Despite the handsome frame courthouse with at least four shanties and an animal pound on the square, some stores and hotels, a handful of basic industries, and a few handsome houses such as those of Wesley Park and George Ensley, the streets were still of mud, notched-eared cows and hogs roamed the town at large, and "night soil" was piled high adjacent to the outhouses.

Auburn Academy. The academy was located on South Van Buren Street between West Twelfth and Thirteenth Streets. The chimneys served wood-burning stoves in each room.

3. Visitors in the Night and Muster Call: The Civil War (1856–1870)

I regret to see that there exists here a very decided disposition to crush every expression of sympathy for the negro race, and I have sometimes fancied I saw a disposition in this Hall to crush to the ground every man who ventured to give utterance to such sympathy. I hope I am mistaken. But against all manifestations of such a feeling have risen to protest, and I do none-the-less earnestly because I am seem to stand alone.

~Edward R. May, DeKalb and Steuben delegate

From 1856 to 1870, the nation was preoccupied with racial tensions, the Civil War, and recovery. James Buchanan was elected President in 1857, followed by Abraham Lincoln in 1861. After Lincoln's assassination on April 14, 1865, his then-unpopular vice president Andrew Johnson ascended to the highest office in the land. Ulysses S. Grant was elected President in 1868, serving two terms until 1877.

In the meantime, life in the Town of Auburn was difficult with little prospect of improvement. The Lakeshore & Michigan Southern Railroad, known as the "Airline Railroad," was completed through DeKalb County, connecting the towns of Butler, Waterloo, Iba (later Sedan), and Corunna with each other and the outside world.

Although it was the seat of county government, Auburn languished in isolation with its mud streets adjacent to the swamps of Cedar Creek, overrun by hogs, cows, and horses. Town leaders were encouraged from time to time by the prospects of a railroad and did what they could to encourage one to pass through by raising money to subscribe to railroad stock, but no railroad was actually built until the Fort Wayne, Jackson & Saginaw was completed in 1870.

A phantom railroad did pass through Auburn, however. Its mission and cargo were more important than a real railroad with iron rails, wood ties, and big iron horses!

As slavery became more oppressive in the South and less acceptable in the North, African Americans sought to escape bondage by heading north to Canada.

There developed a series of routes from south to north that became known as the Underground Railroad. One of the principle organizers was Levi Coffin, a Quaker of Fountain City, Indiana, who was referred to as the "President" of the Underground Railroad. One of the most prominent routes was along the eastern boundary of Indiana, which leads almost directly to the southernmost point of Canada across the border from Detroit.

Many blacks crossed the Ohio River at Cincinnati and then crossed into Indiana and followed the route north into Michigan and then Canada. This route passed through Fort Wayne, Auburn, Angola, and Coldwater, Michigan.

The locations of specific "stations" are difficult to document because the activity was illegal and few details were left in any documented form. The Federal Fugitive Slave Act was enacted in 1850. It compelled state law enforcement officers to assist slave hunters in locating and capturing escaped slaves within their jurisdictions. The 1852 Indiana Constitution and ensuing state legislation forbade African Americans to enter Indiana and made it a crime for any person to assist them to enter or to remain within the state.

Nevertheless, many Hoosiers risked their freedom and property to flaunt the federal and state laws by resisting what they considered the immoral and oppressive institution of slavery. Generally, the fugitive slaves traveled from place to place at night, escorted by local people who were familiar with the territory. They traveled from 6 to 12 miles between stops, depending upon the terrain and weather.

William Cornell, whose home was located at what is now 2132 County Road 68, and his brother Samuel Cornell, whose home was located at what is now 6307 County Road 27, are known to have assisted the fugitives. It is likely that John Morris, an Auburn attorney who lived at 108 North Cedar Street, may have also provided a stop. Another possible site is the home located at 5582 County Road 11A at the northwest quadrant of Interstate 69 and County Road 11A.

The Underground Railroad "conductors" were always ready to receive visitors in the night, to feed and harbor them, and possibly conduct them to the next stop at Waterloo the following night. It is likely that the Underground Railroad operated into the early months of the Civil War.

Otherwise, life remained mundane in Auburn, the monotony broken by an occasional fire such as occurred on January 28, 1856, when the large double-store building of Ralston and Park burned. Auburn had no firefighting apparatus, nor wells, nor cisterns, nor public ladders. The population gathered beyond the radius of the heat and watched the buildings burn to the ground.

The Valentine Weaver Drugstore at the southwest corner of Main and Seventh Streets was threatened, and the citizens attempted to save it by draping the exposed side with carpet that was kept soaked by throwing buckets of water on it. The carpet began steaming and then burst into flames along with the building it was supposed to protect. The Valentine Weaver Drugstore burned to the ground, as did the DeKalb County Treasurer's Office on the northwest corner of the square.

The press and fixtures of the *Democratic Messenger* newspaper were also destroyed, leaving the Town of Auburn and DeKalb County without a newspaper.

The county purchased a vacant building, moved it to the site of the former treasurer's office, and used it to house both the treasurer and recorder. It was common to move buildings in this era. Most structures were not on permanent foundations—just a large rock at each corner—so they were easy to move. The building to be moved was jacked up a bit, the rocks removed, and the building lowered onto round logs that acted as rollers. The building was then pulled by horses or oxen to a new site. Some moving was done by the use of "mud sleds" in the wet seasons. Also, snow and ice over frozen ground provided a slick surface over which a building could be moved; thus, buildings could be recycled.

The first permanent school was finished on January 1, 1857 by O.C. Houghton, who had the low bid of $1,325, including a cupola.

Throughout the pioneer period, crime continued rampant in northeast Indiana. Many criminals from the East found refuge in the area, particularly the Tamarack Swamps of Noble County. Local law enforcement was largely ineffective in fighting crime, especially horse thievery.

In 1852, the Indiana General Assembly passed "An Act to Authorize the formation of companies for the detention and apprehension of Horse Thieves

MORRIS HOUSE. The home of John Morris, an Auburn attorney known to be active in anti-slavery activities, may have been an Underground Railroad station. The house was built c. 1848 and is located at 108 North Cedar Street.

and other felons." Members of these companies had the power of constables. When a member's horse was stolen, all the company's members became a legally constituted posse to chase and capture the thieves.

The first company formed in DeKalb County was the DeKalb County Horse Thief Detecting Company of the State of Indiana on May 28, 1855, at Auburn. Wesley Park was elected Captain and W.W. Griswold, secretary. Its 41 members included S.W. Ralston, James Griswold, James N. Chamberlain, Wesley Park, Isaac Brandt, George Waggoner, W. Waterman, W.W. Griswold, James Draggoo, James T. Bliss, G.G. Griswold, William P. Moore, Christian Sheets, George W. Reed, G.W. Draggoo, S.J. Long, G.V. Widney, Michael Sheets, P.B. Nimmis, Orrin C. Clark, L.G. Holmes, William Clark, A.P. Hartle, P.B. Showers, George Brink, James McClellan, Samuel Husselman, N.H. Matthews, John Ditmar, William McGinnis, Amos Park, William H. Bile, William Grube, Thomas Weldin, Samuel Sanders, Herian Griswold, R.B. Cattin, J.S. Boots, William H. Madden, George Egnew, and H.A. Shull.

Hurrah for Douglas!

(Written for the Occasion.)

"The Douglas" has Come!

TUNE—"Old Dan Tucker."

The gallant Douglas now is here.
He'll make the woolies quake with fear;
They can't conceal their deep chagrin
To see the masses pouring in.
CHORUS—Get out of the way, Old Abe Lincoln,
Your party's spirits fast are sinking;
Get out of the way, we all entreat you,
The Little Giant will surely beat you.

Old Abe may keep a grocery store,
May do to pull a flat-boat oar;
At splitting rails he may succeed;
But he's not one the People need.
CHORUS—Get out of the way, etc.

We want a statesman, sound and true,
To guide our country safely through
The storm which threats to rend apart
The *Union*, dear to every heart.
CHORUS—Get out of the way, etc.

We've here the very man we seek—
Will see his face and hear him speak
This very blessed day, and then
How glum will look the Lincoln men.
CHORUS—Get out of the way, etc.

The weak inventions of the foe
He'll tear to tatters, and will show,
Despite the boasts of Lincoln flats,
Success awaits the Democrats.
CHORUS—Get out of the way, etc.

His principles are known to all;
By them he'll stand, or with them fall;
His motto, and that of our cause,
Is "Equal Rights and Equal Laws."
CHORUS—Get out of the way, etc.

All honor to "the Douglas," then,
And honor to the Douglas men—
The gallant Democrats who stand
The hope and safety of the land.
CHORUS—Get out of the way, etc.

Red, White, and Blue.

For Douglas, the pride of the nation,
The choice of the fearless and free—
We join in a heart-felt ovation,
And he shall our President be!
Our bosoms in throbbing communion,
Remember the statesman so true,
Who sheltered our glorious Union,
And stands by the Red, White, and Blue.

From lands where the millions are yearning
For freedom from tyranny's chain,
Our Douglas in gladness returning,
Beholds dear Columbia again.
His heart beats with freedom's devotion—
His soul is yet steadfast and true;
"He swears to the Union devotion,"
And stands by the Red, White, and Blue.

No factious dissensions shall sever
The bands that our Washington wrought;
"The Union," unchanging forever,
Is shrined in each patriot's thought.
Our love and our faith are not hollow;
In strength they were nourished and grew,
The chief we have chosen we'll follow,
And stand by the Red, White, and Blue.

Our voices are joined in communion—
The stars of our flag are above;
Huzza for Douglas and Union!
Huzza for the man that we love!
The old Union ship which he rides in,
Is staunch in her timbers and true,
And now thro' the state she is gliding;
Her flag is the Red, White, and Blue.

Printed on the Fort Wayne SENTINEL Locomotive Press, in the Procession, at the Grand Douglas Rally, Oct. 2d, 1860.

HURRAH FOR DOUGLAS. This rare broadside was printed on a steam printing press mounted on a wagon being drawn through a parade for Stephen Douglas in Fort Wayne on October 2, 1860. The chorus of the song says, "Get out of the way old Abe Lincoln; your party's spirits are fast sinking; Get out of the way, we all entreat you; the Little Giant will surely beat you!" Douglas, the "Little Giant," carried Auburn over Lincoln in the election.

This company, along with many others, participated in the extra-judicial trial of Gregory McDougal at Ligonier and executed the sentence, "to be hung by the neck until dead," at Diamond Hill on January 28, 1858. A photograph of the proud DeKalb County participants still hangs in the east stairwell of the DeKalb County Courthouse. A full account of vigilante acts appears in *History of the Regulators of Northern Indiana* written by M.H. Mott of Auburn.

Other DeKalb County companies included the Richland Rangers, Fairfield Protectors, Stafford Mutual Protection Association, Concord Rangers, Protection Company of Newville, Union Detectives, DeKalb County Vigilance Committee, Concord Protective Band, Wilmington Center Detectives (1), Wilmington Detectives, Cedar Lake Rangers, St. Joe Protective Association, Detective Association of Butler Township, Concord Regulator Association, Wilmington Center Detectives (2), Keyser Township Detective Association, Jackson Township Detective Association, and Jackson Township Number One Order of Regulators Association.

The game of baseball was "invented" in 1839 by Abner Doubleday in Cooperstown, New York, according to some sources. Others hold that it evolved from the old English game of "rounders." However the game originated, it was being played in Auburn as early as 1856 by the Farmers' Wahalolas.

Word of the nomination of Abraham Lincoln for President by the Republican Party was received in Auburn on May 22, 1860, and was celebrated by a mass meeting on the square with banners, flags, martial music, and bonfires. The crowd was addressed by S.W. Widney and S.B. Ward.

The Democrats were enthralled by their nominee Stephen A. Douglas, described as a "statesman of marked ability, unflinching Jacksonian firmness and an undaunted advocate of self-government." A large campaign meeting was held at Auburn with W.S. "Popgun" Smith, a popular Fort Wayne orator, as principle speaker.

W.H. McIntosh observed:

> As the campaign drew to a close, politics became the absorbing issue; a grand demonstration was made by the democracy at Waterloo. Hickory poles were raised amid cheers from the throngs of spectators, many ladies carrying a beautiful banner made and owned by Mr. M.F. Pearce, of Auburn, marched in a long procession to a stand for speakers whence they were eloquently addressed by Judge Lowry and P. Hinkel. While political fever ran high personal, municipal and county interests held even tenor. The multitude did not realize the gravity of the issues involved and very few anticipated actual war.

Lincoln carried DeKalb County by a vote of 1,474 to 1,323, but lost Auburn by a vote of 129 to 92.

While the seeds of civil strife were sprouting on the national scene, the people of Auburn were preoccupied by those things that affected their immediate lives and comfort, particularly the building of sidewalks. The Auburn town board decided that sidewalks on lots fronting Main Street on the square were to be 10 feet wide, along with those on Fourth and Ninth Streets. All others were to be 4 feet. The sidewalks were all made of rough sawn planks.

Another great need was "cross walks" on the muddy streets. These were built across Main Street at Fourth, Fifth, Sixth, Seventh, and Eighth Streets. They were 2 feet wide and made of 3-inch planks. They were to be installed as close to the surface as possible because they had to be crossed by those driving wagons or buggies on the street.

The *New Era* newspaper reported the following on May 16, 1860:

> Our sidewalks are now fast being built, the public square will soon be enclosed in a neat fence, and our citizens are painting and fixing up generally. Saturday is a busy day. Nearly every business house in town has been crowded with customers from all parts of the county. Auburn is coming out. The weather is fair, roads are good, and farmers are having a splendid time planting their corn and doing all kind of outside work.

The picture gallery located "opposite Sander's Store" was operated by Jerome Gallahan, "where ambrotypes of superior execution were taken in clouded as well as clear weather, and are still preserved as priceless momentos of departed kindred and friends."

Many other businesses had located in Auburn by 1860. J. Dutch Davis conducted a Hardware and Stove Emporium, the predecessor of Davis Pioneer Hardware at 203 South Main Street, and Valentine Weaver's Drug Store at the southwest corner of Main and Seventh Streets was acquired by Dr. W.M. Mercer and his brother for the sale of drugs and medicine.

A Mr. Bues of England entered the trade of millinery and dressmaking in Auburn after serving a full apprenticeship in the city of London. He invited patrons to his shop and advertised that he was "in weekly receipt of New York styles." William H. Dills was the first insurance agent in Auburn, representing the Home Insurance Company of New York. Egbert B. Mott, Esquire, began selling real estate along with his practice of law. He had over 2,000 acres of DeKalb County real estate for sale in 1860. George Wagoner had a "home like" restaurant and dealt in family groceries and refreshments. George W. Taylor was a tailor of men's and boy's clothing. S.S. Ford sold his boot and shoe business to C.S. Hare. Samuel Sander conducted a general store under the name "Farmer's Exchange Store" at the corner of Main and Fourth Streets. Stiefel and Wolf advertised "selling on the cost" and great bargains could be had at their expense if the customer acted promptly.

Edward Eldridge operated a saloon in downtown Auburn for many years, and John Butt had the DeKalb Saloon, which carried wine, liquor, and cigars. His poetic ads included stanzas like these:

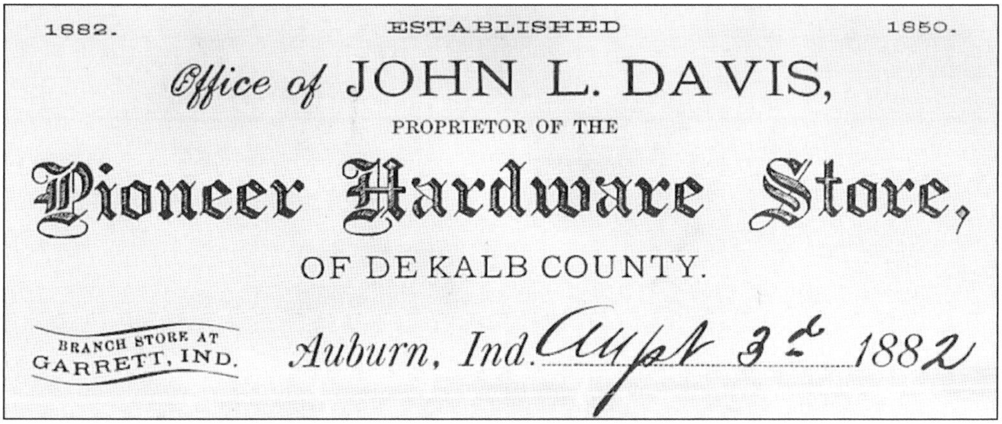

1882. ESTABLISHED 1850.

Office of JOHN L. DAVIS,

PROPRIETOR OF THE

Pioneer Hardware Store,

OF DE KALB COUNTY.

BRANCH STORE AT GARRETT, IND.

Auburn, Ind. Aug 3d 1882

PIONEER HARDWARE STORE LETTERHEAD. Pioneer Hardware Store was established in 1850 and is still in business at the same location as Auburn City Hardware.

Should a party of friends for an evening drop in,
Just send for a dozen of Butt's Brandy and Gin.

If the earth should ever be flooded again,
Let's hope all the rain will be Butt's Brandy and Gin.

Three hack lines carried salesmen in and out of Auburn, as well as deposits of money to banks at Waterloo and Kendallville, and passengers to and from railroad connections at Waterloo and Fort Wayne. James Griswold operated a daily hack from Auburn to Waterloo, Butt and Darrow ran a hack every other day to Fort Wayne, and R. Squires ran the popular Auburn, Angola, & Coldwater Hack Line.

Interest in the history of DeKalb County was awakened by the publication of *Pioneer Sketches of DeKalb County* by S.W. Widney in 1859. Although the county was scarcely 25 years old, the people recognized that they themselves were pioneers and that their history should be preserved. An Old Settlers Association held its first meeting in September 1860. Wesley Park was chairman of the Central Committee, which included Lewis Blair, S.W. Widney, S.W. Sprott, and D.N. Altenberg. The General Committee was composed of a representative from each township. Membership was limited to those who had settled prior to 1840, later extended to 1845. The Old Settlers met annually for many years. In 1892, W.H. McIntosh stated, "An historical society ought to be organized in connection with the old settler organization and the narratives of pioneers yet living would give present pleasure and prove of lasting importance to generations yet to be."

The story of the Civil War is familiar to all Americans, but what effect did it have on Auburn and our ancestors? After the election of Abraham Lincoln in 1860, a showdown between slave and nonslave interests was forced. Soon, Mississippi, Florida, Alabama, Georgia, Louisiana, Texas, Virginia, Arkansas, South Carolina, and Tennessee seceded from the Union.

LAKESHORE DEPOT. The Fort Wayne, Jackson & Saginaw Railroad was later acquired by the Lakeshore & Michigan Southern Railroad and was popularly known as the "Lakeshore." The depot was located north of West Seventh Street. The railroad trackage is now owned and operated by the Auburn Port Authority.

On April 12, 1861, Fort Sumter was fired upon by Confederate forces. News of this startling event was received by telegraph operators on the Lakeshore & Michigan Southern Railroad at Butler, Waterloo, and Corunna, and the news traveled fast to Auburn. The tranquil lives of our Auburn ancestors were to be interrupted for several difficult years. McIntosh observed:

> Keenly alive to the gravity of pending events, the citizens of Auburn, in common with those of ten thousands of northern towns and cities eagerly caught up every item of political import while a chaotic confusion of sentiment included opinions ranging from the most radical, to the ultra of conservatism. But when the tocsin of war was sounded by secession guns in Charleston harbor, DeKalb county stood not idly in the background although few counties in the northern part of Indiana, met more opposition of various character.

On April 15, 1861, President Lincoln issued a call for 75,000 volunteers to serve for three months and be sent to the states that had seceded, in order to execute the laws of the United States.

Most Civil War troops were volunteers. By an Act of Congress on July 22, 1863, all volunteers for one year were given a bounty of $100. Re-enlisting veterans received a bounty of $400. During 1864 and 1865, a bounty of $100 was paid for one year, $200 for two years, and $300 for three years.

Two drafts were required in Indiana to fill quotas set by the war department for each county and township. Those which complied with the quotas were not subject to the draft. The first draft was pursuant to the Conscription Act of Congress on July 17, 1862. The period of service was not to exceed nine months. All able-bodied men between the ages of 18 and 45 were subject to draft.

Governor Oliver Morton appointed a commissioner for each county, who in turn appointed a deputy for each township. The deputy was responsible for taking a poll of each man who was eligible. A commutation could be purchased for $300 and substitutes could be hired by those who could afford it.

A total of 1,862 men volunteered from DeKalb County and 272 were drafted, for a grand total of 2,134 men. In 1860, the population of the county was 13,865, creating a conscription rate for the county of 15.39 percent.

Ironically, the first DeKalb County war casualty occurred at Waterloo. On July 10, 1861, the people of Waterloo gathered at the depot to honor the men who were leaving to join the first company of DeKalb County volunteers. A cannon was being fired in honor of the volunteers who were leaving on the express train at 3:50 p.m. Two rounds had been fired, but the third one was reserved until the departure of the train.

The cannon had been heavily charged and was wadded to within a few inches of the muzzle with green leather shavings from the tannery. As the train pulled out, the cannon was discharged. The result was a terrific explosion, bursting the cannon into thousands of pieces and scattering the fragments of iron in all directions, over houses and treetops, and carrying some pieces as far as 80 rods.

John Henry Shoemaker of Smithfield Township, who had assisted in loading the gun, applied the match and was struck by a piece of iron that cut a gash in his side and completely severed his spinal cord. He died instantly. As he was about to fire the piece, he was heard to remark, "Those boys over there," pointing to a crowd at the depot, "said they would not touch it off for five hundred dollars." In another instant, he was dead. Although there were many narrow escapes, remarkably, no other person in the crowed was injured.

Hundreds of troop trains passed through DeKalb County, carrying young men for quick training and then on to the front. Some of these trains stopped for DeKalb County soldiers. Munition trains also passed through the county. The *Waterloo Press* reported the following on September 21, 1861:

> Two special trains, laden with cannon, powder balls, shells, etc. have passed here this week. The cannon were of large size and destined for fortifying the Mississippi Valley. The following is the bill of goods: Ten 64 pounders; twenty 32 pounders; 2,467 32 pound balls; 147 64 pound balls; and sixty-four 96 pound balls; an aggregate of 91,840 pounds of shot, shell and ball.

The first company of 88 men raised entirely from DeKalb County volunteers was organized by Captain Cyrus Hawley as Company H of the 30th Infantry Regiment. Company H was the pride of DeKalb County and counted among its members some of our best citizens. They called themselves the DeKalb County Guards and were presented with a banner by the ladies of Auburn before leaving for Camp Allen in Fort Wayne in September 1861.

Companies were also raised by Captain Wesley Park and Captain George W. Merrill. Merrill's was Company F and Park's was Company K, both attached to the 44th Indiana Infantry Regiment.

Not all citizens of DeKalb County were loyal to the Union, however. Some were of southern extraction and openly opposed the war. John and Samuel Husselman were brothers who came to DeKalb County in 1839. They were very close for many years, but differed strongly with each other in connection with the Civil War. John was pro-Union and Samuel was pro-South. They never reconciled their differences and to this day it is said that descendants of John are Republicans and that descendants of Samuel are Democrats.

The Coburntown Church of Christ excommunicated several of its members who were Southern sympathizers. Most were later reinstated to membership.

Typical of other areas, most of DeKalb County's quota was supplied by volunteers. The county paid bounties to volunteers in the amount of $126,500.50, and the townships paid $12,600, for a total of $139,100.50. This would equal about $75 per volunteer in addition to the enlistment bounties paid by the federal government. Relief paid to the families of soldiers was $24,481.63, paid by both the township and the county, for an average of about $11.50 per family.

Wilmington, Stafford, and Newville Townships furnished their quotas by volunteers. Newville had 170 eligible young men and supplied 40 volunteers, or 23.5 percent. The numbers drafted in the first draft in other townships were: Troy, 8; Franklin, 22; Richland, 41; Union, 2; Jackson, 12; Butler, 8; Concord, 1; Smithfield, 25; and Fairfield, 30; for a total of 149.

It is interesting to note that traditionally Republican townships had more volunteers while the traditionally Democratic townships had more drafted, perhaps indicating the degree of Southern sympathy in the latter townships, or perhaps the relative affluence of the residents.

Auburn townsmen were very patriotic in the face of the threat to their treasured Union. On the Fourth of July, 1861, a large celebration was held. At daybreak, a salute of 34 shots was fired under the direction of Thomas Weldon. The Stars and Stripes were raised at the 17th shot. That year, there were 34 states—17 remained in the Union and the balance were Confederate. McIntosh described the events of the day:

> The procession marched to the grove where Rev. James Hadsell officiated as Chaplain, James Colgrove read the Declaration of Independence and following the singing by the glee club of the Star Spangled Banner, and the Red, White and Blue, most appropriate and deservedly popular

patriotic songs, the Hon. A.M Latta, of Ligonier was introduced as the orator of the day.

In this connection, the following expression has been proved prophetic: "Within a few years there will be no honored silver hairs to remind us of this natal day. Great changes will take place and when this rebellion is put down, another day may be placed upon the national calendar for us to hold in grateful remembrance to awaken pure feelings of patriotism and freedom."

The women of Auburn formed the Soldiers' Aid Society. As soldiers left town, the ladies provided a "bounteous dinner" for them. They also prepared delicacies for the sick and boxes of baked goods and clothing for the men at war.

The venerable entrepreneur Wesley Park became a suttler after sustaining an injury. A suttler was a private merchant authorized by the government to sell sundries to the soldiers, such as tobacco, candy, liquor, and other incidentals. His sons A.B. Park and Henry Park assisted him. The Park father and sons followed the 44th Indiana and it was said that their dealing was always "honorable and generous."

A future judge of the DeKalb Circuit Court, Robert W. McBride (1882–1888), enlisted in 1863 as a member of the Union Light Guard of Ohio, organized by Governor David Tod of Ohio as an elite volunteer calvary unit. This unit, mounted on elegant black horses, was assigned to provide an escort for President Lincoln whenever he traveled from the White House. The President and his

UNION CIVIL WAR VETERANS. A group of Civil War veterans is shown in uniform outside the 1865 courthouse.

family frequently spent weekends at the Soldiers' Home Cottage, located in a wooded area near the Capitol. While there, the President frequently rode about the grounds alone in the evening.

One evening, around 11 p.m., the guards heard a gunshot. Shortly thereafter, the bareheaded President rode up and reported that his horse had been frightened at the sound of the gunshot and jerked in such a way that his hat had fallen off. Corporal McBride and a sentry were dispatched to search for the President's trademark stovepipe hat. They found it with a bullet hole through the crown. When the hat was returned to Lincoln, he made a humorous remark about the ability of the marksman and admonished McBride that he wanted nothing reported about the incident. Judge McBride reported his experiences in a book he wrote in 1911 entitled *Lincoln's Body Guard: The Union Light Guard of Ohio, with Some Personal Recollections of Abraham Lincoln.*

Judge Egbert B. Mott's son Sheridan E. Mott, who had joined him in the practice of law in 1861, was mustered into Company A of the 88th Indiana Infantry on July 18, 1862. He died March 18, 1865 of wounds sustained at the Battle of Bentonville, North Carolina. His body was returned to Auburn and was interred in the Mott Family Cemetery on North Main Street.

Even though the bitter war was raging in the South, life continued on a normal basis in Auburn. The hotel located west of the Swineford House facing Van Buren Street was taken over by John Butt and refitted with new furniture from

NORTH SIDE OF SQUARE. *The board fence around the square is in the foreground, and the Odd Fellows Building is on the right. Merchants' signs include Excelsior Hardware, Auburn Art Gallery, Books, Watches and Jewelry, and Printing Office. A man in the right foreground holds a tree out of the way.*

the "cabinet warerooms" of the Ettingers. The grand opening was celebrated by "old fashioned entertainment" on February 15, 1861, consisting of a ball and supper. Music was supplied by Forsythe's Band.

Auburn merchants realized that their prosperity depended largely on the prosperity of the farmers of the county. They organized the DeKalb Agricultural Society at a meeting held at the courthouse on January 21, 1861. A fair was held October 4 and 5, 1861 at Auburn. Awards were given to James Griswold for blooded horses; B.F. Greenwood, light draft and saddle horses; J.J. Holmes, heavy draught horses; E. White, blooded cattle; B. Altenberg, cross-blooded cattle; J.M. Brumbeck, the best yoke of work cattle; A.M. Brumbeck, long wooled sheep; J.P. Boyer, fine wooled sheep; W. Griswold, hogs; and J. Willis for wagon and buckboard. In the culinary department, Mrs. T. Weldin took first on preserves, Mr. H. Willis took first on currant wine and jellies, and Mrs. C. Sheets took first on loaf of bread.

The Democratic Party was the big winner in the fall 1861 election. Despite the war, or perhaps because of it, the Town of Auburn was becoming more prosperous. Joseph Loveland, editor of the *New Era*, editorialized:

> Business wears a pleasing countenance, Merchants, tradesmen and manufacturers of all branches have promise of brisk and heavy trade. Many of our merchants are already preparing for customary eastern visits and a general felling of confidence prevailes with business of men of all classes and heavy investments are before our townspeople. The sound of the mechanic's hammer and the hum of machinery in the manufacturers, greet us again. Store houses and ware rooms are being crowded with goods, wares and customers and prosperity and happiness abound in every home in our village.

Loveland's optimism was confirmed with the reliable testimony of S.W. Ralston, who said, "Never before in the history of our country has the labor of the husbandman been more bountifully rewarded than in the present. DeKalb County is behind no section in regard to crops and will in time be known as the garden of Indiana." There was still much to be done to bring Auburn up to standard as a town, though. The Bolinger Fanning Mill Factory burned, and there was still no fire department or equipment to fight fire.

The fence around the square was repaired and a hitching rail installed along the west side of Main Street on the square. A feed lot was established on the south side of the square for visitors to leave their horses while they shopped. A public well with a hand pump was installed on the north side of the square.

The Auburn Brass Band was organized in 1862 and provided "nocturnal serenades" under the direction of Professor Charles Struby.

After only 20 years, the frame courthouse had become inadequate for the growing county. The handsome little building did not contain the space needed for county offices. The extra offices around the square were small, unsightly, and inefficient.

The population of DeKalb County had grown from about 3,000 in 1840 to 13,880 in 1860. This was a prosperous time. A new courthouse was in order.

The plans and specifications for the new courthouse were approved by the Board of Commissioners on April 20, 1863. The contract, actually let on June 4 of that year, was awarded to Alpheus Wheelock, John McKay, and William Valleu for the sum of $23,372.

Brick used in the building was manufactured locally at the Woodbury Farm located three-quarters of a mile east of Auburn. Within one month, the foundation pits had been excavated and stone for the walls delivered to the square. The foundation was completed by September 10, 1863, and the cornerstone laid on the northeast corner of the foundation walls with appropriate ceremonies. On July 1, 1863, a bell weighing 600 pounds and cast at the Buckeye Bell Foundry in Cincinnati, Ohio, was brought by train to Auburn.

The new courthouse was ready for occupancy before the December 1, 1864 contract completion date. The surplus brick was used to construct a large brick house at the corner of Tenth and Main Streets, which at that time was known as the John Henry property. The first floor of the courthouse building was divided into four offices, each 21 by 24 feet. The entrance was via a hallway extending east and west through the building with large double doors of iron and wood at each end. The windows were secured by inside iron shutters, and each office was provided with fireproof iron-door vaults. The courtroom was on the second floor and originally measured 64 by 60 feet, with grand and petit jury rooms on the west end. The roof was of Vermont slate laid on wood lath. At the west end, there was an octagonal tower 22 feet in diameter and 80 feet high. From the second story, a spiral staircase led to a balcony that commanded a bird's-eye view of the Town of Auburn and surrounding areas. From the summit of the dome extended a flagstaff that supported a copper eagle at an elevation of 115 feet.

Before construction was started on the new courthouse, the old building was moved approximately 40 feet north of its original location to make room for its successor. The last court session held in the old structure was during the spring term of 1864. In September 1864, the old building was sold to Daniel Altenburg for the sum of $25. He partially dismantled it and removed everything of value. This was near the end of the Civil War, and when news reached Auburn that Richmond, capital of the waning Confederacy, had been captured by the Union Army, a huge crowd of local citizens congregated around the square for a public celebration. It was suggested that a bonfire would be appropriate, to which Altenburg replied, "If you want to make a bonfire, you may burn the old courthouse." He was soon taken at his word and the old building, for years the scene of local justice, found a glorious end in the blazing of a national celebration.

Some thought the plans for the new courthouse were too grand and the tower unnecessary. Alpheas Wheelock, the builder, was very patriotic and a member of the Union League. The *Auburn Daily Courier* reported an interview with Wheelock on June 10, 1910, in which he said, "Make a tower and hang Old Glory at its top, and when the boys in faded blue return they will be greeted by the good old stars

1865 DEKALB COUNTY COURTHOUSE. This view is taken from the southwest and shows the cannon. The tower was an Auburn landmark.

and stripes!" This declaration inspired the patriotism of many, and was the "cry" from morning until night, until the tower was assured.

The tower was long a landmark that could be seen from a considerable distance as one approached Auburn. Its cast iron balcony provided a platform high above the ground for orators and for band concerts. No doubt those soldiers who came home alive saw the red, white, and blue flying high over their old hometown.

Charles A. Munn operated the Auburn Male and Female Institute. In addition to other subjects, the Institute offered German, French, Latin, and Greek at the tuition of $6.50 per 12-week term. The school was widely attended, particularly by students from other towns and townships surrounding Auburn.

On February 6, 1864, the 44th Indiana, Company K, discharged 220 men, but each re-enlisted for another term. The 44th had fought gallantly in the Battles of Donelson, Shiloh, Stone River, and Chickamauga.

The Civil War ended at Appomatox on April 9, 1865, and reconstruction began both as a natural consequence and as a political purpose. Soldiers returned forever sobered by their war experiences. They gradually assimilated into Auburn's fabric and soon became a political and social force as a group. Organized first as the Union Soldiers Association (USA) and then as the Grand Army of the Republic (GAR), the Civil War veterans continued to be a major force into the next century.

McIntosh, writing in 1892, felt that the people of Auburn had a collective inferiority complex concerning their town:

MAIN STREET, LOOKING NORTH. In this early photograph of the west and north sides of the square, the streets are still dirt. The board sidewalks appear on the left and right, and the brick buildings still stand.

Auburn seemed to be and was by comparison a backward place, her people appeared to rest content with their quiescent condition while Waterloo City increased with gratifying speed and became the commercial metropolis of the county. The people of Auburn were influenced by a combination of habit and necessity to wait for opportunity and to let events decide the future. The war having closed, population was augmented by return of soldiers and the sterling qualities that had made their services valuable to the country, were turned to account in civil life and this community was benefited largely by the vigor they infused into all channels of trade and industry. It was then a familiar sight to see groups of veterans still in their worn blue uniforms congregated at times near the public square to exchange greetings and relate experiences. At more frequent intervals now strangers dropped in, some to chance success and meet failure, others to study the possibilities of the locality, determine to stay and during the years that followed, they enhanced their own welfare while adding to the material interests of the town. The record of business changes for the year is not extended, but such improvements as were attempted were in the right direction. Time and again in these annals, we have seen some retire from their pursuits and others hopefully take their places, many to fail in their turn, a few to meet a reasonable prosperity.

> Looking at our streets this season of 1892, remembering the labor and material expended upon them, we may well believe the statement of Mr. Coe, in 1865. "Our streets," said he, "are filthy, the alleys are obstructed, they offend the senses and endanger the health of people. The streets need cleaning, the sidewalks are out of repair, the dilapidated conditions of the old fence about the public square has become an eye sore to resident and stranger, visitor and we are wearied of seeing dog fennel per-empting ground which might be a beautiful park." The criticism was timely. The streets in the spring season were almost impassable. Horses and vehicles sank deep in the mud churned by hoof and wheel into the consistency of sticky paste. Deep holes formed in the roadway and through these teams struggled or in attempted avoidance, encroached upon the domain of sidewalk. Summer came and cross streets were beautiful in growth of grass, but along the traveled roadways, the firm surface was covered with dust that swept in clouds against dwellings and annoyed passers by. In the fall, some effort was made to remedy these faults and some of the few narrow, wooden sidewalks were repaired but there was not system and little appearance of the public spirit now existing.

With the bleak assessment of the collective mindset of the people of Auburn, the town began its own reconstruction. A group of citizens—S.W. Sprott, John Brandon, Christian Buss, Thomas D. Gross, Sylvester Kutzner, Lewis Bower, Joseph D. Davis, and Christian Sheets—incorporated the Auburn Woolen Manufacturing Company, capitalized at $20,000.

A building three stories high and 42 feet by 62 feet was built by Francis Picker, mason, and Thomas Baldock, carpenter. There was an 18-foot, one-story annex along the entire east side for a steam engine and boiler. An adjacent dye house was also erected to hold the necessary dye tubs and piping to the boiler. There were 12 large looms, all powered by the steam engine.

Joseph McKay was foreman, George Miller was spinner, and Henry Kelly was engineer to operate the boiler and steam engine.

The opening of the factory was described by McIntosh:

> Every thing being ready, on August 2, the furnace fires were lighted, steam was raised in the boiler and the machinery set in motion. Mr. Sprott one of the founders of the mill and secretary of the company invited patronage and soon large quantities of wool began to come in. It was pride and curiosity of townspeople to see the work of carding, weaving, fulling, and different processes from the fleece to the excellent cloth made and it was peculiarly, but none the less truthfully stated that "the farmers of DeKalb county could now spin their yarn, pay their taxes, do their courting and get their grists all at the county seat." . . . the woolen factory was an Auburn industry of which its population was

> proud. From time to time improvements were effected and with its 220 spinets, its looms and other machinery, its capacity was equal to the manufacture into cloth of 100 lbs. of wool per day.

Most Civil War veterans had returned to Auburn by June 1865. There was general sentiment that their return should be acknowledged by a Fourth of July celebration on the square. A committee was formed and a grand celebration planned. John P. Widney was the president of the day, and Robert Lowry and James I. Best were orators.

Bells were rung all day, anvil discharges were made (a charge of gunpowder was laced under an anvil and then lit; the anvil, weighing over 300 pounds, was shot into the air), guns were fired, and the Auburn Brass Band serenaded from the balustrade of the courthouse cupola. A Liberty Pole 160 feet high was raised from the center of the west side of the square. A large flag was "run up and unfurled in the morning breeze."

Soldiers in full uniform formed a procession to march to the grove located on Main Street between 14th and 15th Streets. A large carry-in meal was enjoyed. The group then adjourned to another grove on the west edge of town where a declaration was read by John B. Morrison and a patriotic oration was made by Judge Robert Lawry of Goshen.

The day concluded with a grand ball held on the new floor of the Auburn Woolen Mills with music furnished by Miller and Hoover of Waterloo. Then followed a supper at the Weaver House.

In December of 1866, a few of the leading citizens of Auburn realized the need for a good road between Waterloo City and Auburn. If Auburn did not have a railroad, at least a good road should be built to connect the town with the railroad at Waterloo. J.L. Worden, S.W. Ralston, Edward Eldridge, L. Rainier, and Lewis J. Blair organized "The Auburn and Waterloo City Plank Road Company" and secured the authority of the DeKalb County Commissioners to build a plank road over the existing road (part of the Fort Wayne–Coldwater Road). The commissioners required that the plank road be started within one year and completed within two years. Presumably, a toll would have been charged to defer the cost of the construction and maintenance of the plank road, but for unknown reasons, it was never built.

The Civil War created an era of inflation and a good business climate. The years following the war saw a gradual decline in economic conditions. The lack of a bank in Auburn contributed to its decline, as did the generally unstable currency. There was no central national or state banking system. Currency was issued by individual banks, which might or might not be redeemed upon presentation. Gold and silver were scarce. Some banks even issued fractional currency due to the lack of coins. Some merchants issued their own coins known as Civil War Trade Tokens. These coins were redeemable at their own stores for merchandise and were often traded between townsmen in order to get a token for a store from which they needed to purchase a special item.

This was a dark era for Auburn and it rekindled another move to shift the county seat to the more prosperous Waterloo City. In 1868, some hope emerged with word that the Fort Wayne, Jackson & Saginaw Railroad was projecting its line through or near Auburn. The Auburn Town Board allowed the claim of L.D. Rainier in the amount of $27 for entertaining "railroad men" from Fort Wayne.

Auburn businessmen were determined that the railroad would be built through the town and launched a campaign to get this done. A committee was formed, which appointed W.H. Dills and T.D. Gross to solicit subscriptions at a 1.25 percent commission. The subscriptions were conditional upon the railroad's being built through or within one-half mile of the town. By January 4, 1869, conditional subscriptions totaling nearly $30,000 had been secured. It was felt that this princely sum would be sufficient to induce the "railroad men" to consider Auburn favorably.

Within the next several months, additional subscriptions of $10,000 were secured with another $10,000 promised. The zeal of T.D. Gross was rewarded by his being elected to be assistant treasurer of the railroad. W.H. McIntosh completed the story:

> It was said in the *LaGrange Democrat*: "Is it possible citizens of Auburn are so dead to their interest as to let the road go around them and forever

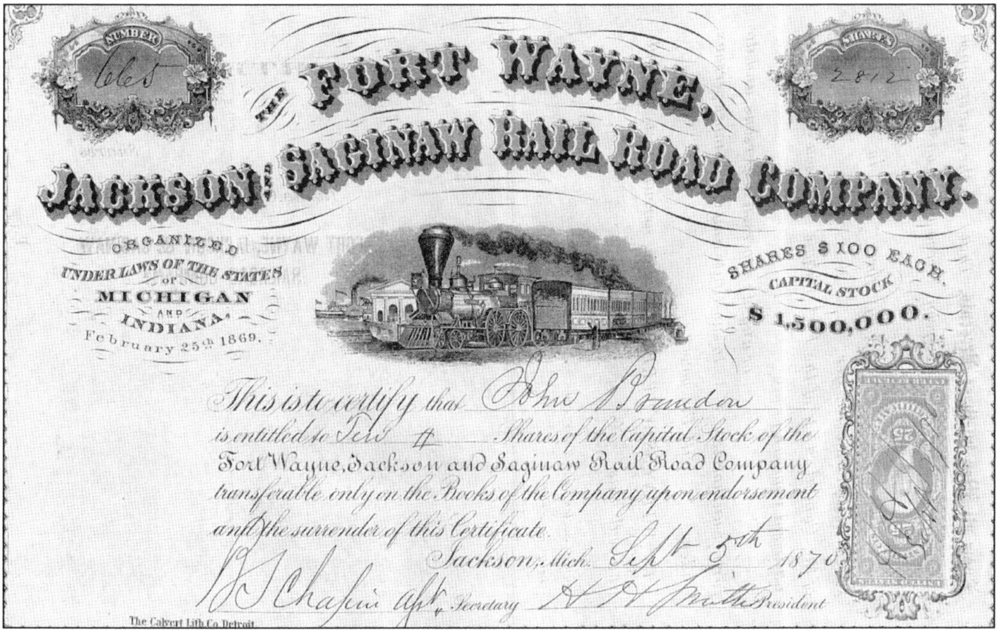

FORT WAYNE, JACKSON & SAGINAW RAILROAD STOCK CERTIFICATE. The Fort Wayne, Jackson & Saginaw Railroad was the first railroad actually built through Auburn. The stock was sold for $100 per share. The stamp on the lower right corner of this certificate is a U.S. Revenue stamp, which indicated that the stock tax had been paid.

> lose the only opportunity of securing a railroad to their village?" Had the editor visited Auburn he would have seen no want of vitality among the townspeople but rather a deep, determination to win at all hazards. He would have seen them, calling meetings to discuss the prospects reporting progress and encouraging further efforts and he would have learned that the all-absorbing topic of conversation on the streets and in the business places was the railroad and its assumed advantages to town and country.

At a special session of the Board of County Commissioners held February 4, 1869, a strong effort was made to get aid from the county. The columns of the existing newspapers in Auburn and Waterloo City contained long letters presenting arguments in favor of the movement and calling for a popular vote, and there were answering letters from those opposing an appropriation, while a remonstrance was presented from Fairfield township bearing 147 signatures. The plea for help was ably presented by Messrs. Smith, Cary Evans, G.W. McConnel, T.R. Dickinson, W.H. Dills, and others, but unsuccessfully.

The county was known to be in debt. There was urgent need for new bridges and a home for the indigent. These among other considerations influenced the officials, who found the people restive under the losses from the robbery of the DeKalb County treasurer's office and consequent futile, expensive litigation to

CREAMERY AT AUBURN JUNCTION. The railroads provided transportation for farmers to sell their products in regional and national markets.

leave the matter of subscriptions to individual enterprise. Those who expected to profit should be the first to pay.

In no way disheartened by failure to obtain aid from the county, although in taxation alone the money would have been eventually repaid, the people of the two towns, working together for a common object, raised their subscriptions to the sum of $112,000. This large amount was contributed, not alone by the townspeople, but material aid was given by farmers residing along and near the line of the road. A marked feature of the donations was the public spirit of the poorer class, who in some instances signed more than they were able to pay in money or labor and met their installments at considerable personal self-denial.

One person of modest means of Waterloo was unable to pay his installments when due. Suit was averted only by his wife's taking two tie contractors named George and Jacob to board, and applying their money on the subscription.

On February 24, 1869, stockholders of the railroad held a meeting to vote upon terms of consolidation with the Michigan Company. The location of the road through Auburn and Waterloo was determined. At one time, the line was expected to pass along the east side of Auburn, perhaps occupying Cedar Street and thereby establishing the junction at the Wabash grounds at the junction of Ensley Avenue, instead of a mile westward. But this was not to be. The line approaching the town from the north was deflected westward and the depot placed near the freight house on the western terminus of Sixth Street. In this vicinity, a tract was platted as Gross & Dills Addition and the lots long since fully occupied by neat new buildings, the homes of townsmen.

All difficulties were surmounted, prospects brightened, and ground was broken for the railroad with appropriate ceremonies on March 29, 1869, in the city park in Fort Wayne. Speeches of the kind usual to such occasions were made by officials and soon contractors were at work clearing the roadway and preparing the grade. Messrs. Gross and Gloyd, contractors for sections in DeKalb County, began work in June 1869 and, by the middle of August 1869, had a large force upon the line between Auburn and Waterloo. A "sink hole" was found on this section. Several others were found to exist in the county. One on the Lakeshore Railroad east of Sedan proved a formidable obstacle in the construction of that road. Much labor was required and a vast amount of filling before track could be laid. On one occasion, the morning light disclosed the absences of track, ties, and rails that had sunk during the night. It was a long time before the spot was filled so as to stand firm and secure.

The railroad was completed in 1870. The first train passed through Auburn on October 5, 1870, loaded with railroad officials and dignitaries from Fort Wayne headed north to the Michigan State Farm at Jackson. The Fort Wayne, Jackson & Saginaw Depot was located on a 5-acre tract north of West Seventh Street. The depot was located on the east side of the tracks between Sixth and Seventh Streets. A freight house was on the west side of the tracks just south of West Seventh Street.

In 1872, a plank sidewalk was built from Main Street along the north side of West Seventh Street all the way to the Fort Wayne, Jackson & Saginaw Depot, "which was a boon to the pedestrians in relief from mud and water," according to W.H. McIntosh.

Auburn pioneers were saddened to learn that the town's founder, Wesley Park, died of typhoid fever on August 11, 1868 at Graham, Missouri and was buried at the Prairie Home Cemetery. He was born November 11, 1811 in Licking County, Ohio and had married Sophia Jugman of Ohio on January 2, 1833. She died on March 26, 1856 and is interred at the Evergreen Cemetery. After her death, Park married Laura Pembroke in August 1858. She died March 11, 1862 and is also interred at the Evergreen Cemetery. Park's third marriage was to Delana Aldrich Beecher. In June 1865, they moved to Andrew County, Missouri, where he entered several hundred acres of land from the United States government and founded the Methodist church and school. A memorial to Wesley Park was erected in the Evergreen Cemetery by the Auburn Lions Club in 1956.

WESLEY PARK. This only known photograph of Wesley Park has been digitally enhanced. It appeared in a 1956 article in the Evening Star.

4. Rails, Wagons, and Buggies:
The Industrial Revolution (1871–1899)

. . . the importance of those men who had the foresight to perceive and who labored so strenuously to secure our present railroad facilities, becomes apparent and claims recognition from old time residents and subsequent arrivals.

~W.H. McIntosh, *Auburn Courier*, August 2, 1893

Auburn finally had its railroad.

The Auburn & Eel River Railroad, later to be known as the Logansport & Northern Indiana Railroad, had been projected from Logansport to Auburn in the early 1850s. Surveyors had platted and staked the route from Logansport to Butler in 1855 with plans to extend the line to Detroit sometime in the future. Yet, no railroad was built and the right-of-way remained only a projected paper dream of the promoters and the towns along its path.

Another railroad—the Detroit, Eel River & Illinois Railroad—was incorporated on November 4, 1868 and obtained the right-of-way of the Logansport & Northern Indiana Railroad. Construction started in 1872 and, by the end of that year, was completed from Denver, Indiana to Auburn. The segment from Auburn to Butler was completed in October 1873. This railroad provided a link to the Lakeshore & Michigan Southern Railroad at Butler and connected with several other railroads between Auburn and Logansport.

The Detroit, Eel River & Illinois was foreclosed upon in 1877 and its assets sold to the organizers of the Eel River Railroad, who in turn leased the assets and trackage to railroad magnate Jay Gould's expanding Wabash, St. Louis, & Pacific Railroad. This provided a through route from St. Louis to Detroit with many connections in between.

Now Auburn had two railroads with the prospect of still another! In 1872, the Baltimore & Ohio Railroad chose a route through DeKalb County for the extensive expansion of its line from Pittsburgh to Chicago. All DeKalb County had to do was provide a 66-foot right-of-way through the county. No cash investment or subscriptions were required, as had been the case with the Fort Wayne, Jackson & Saginaw and the Logansport & Northern Indiana Railroads.

It was thought for some time that Auburn would become a division point for the railroad. A "division point" was the location on the railroad where crews and engines were changed. In anticipation of this, Jacob Stamets platted Stamets Addition south of Auburn and adjacent to the railroad. He also built a hotel to serve the railroad near where he thought the depot would be located.

Land acquisition negotiations broke down, however, and railroad officials sent Washington Cowen, the father of John W. Cowen, chief attorney for the railroad, to pose as a farmer from Ohio looking for farmland west of Auburn. He was able to purchase a tract of 604 acres of land to become Garrett, after the land was platted by the Baltimore Improvement Company, a subsidiary of the Baltimore & Ohio Railroad.

Garrett was platted by railroad officials as a model division point for railroad purposes. Ample space along the track was reserved for a depot, shops, roundhouse, and water tanks. The business district was near the railroad. There were ample residential lots for railroad workers. The original town was located south of the tracks, rather than on both sides, so workers would not be delayed by trains blocking the tracks. The railroad profited from the sale of lots and from the sale of lumber and materials for building houses.

The location of the division point at Garrett was to have an effect on Auburn for many years in that it attracted many Eastern European workers with skills that would become useful to the automotive industry.

While the three railroads came through or near Auburn, they intersected about a mile southwest of the courthouse square at what was to become Auburn Junction. At this point, the Baltimore & Ohio Railroad built a "Union Depot," which served the Baltimore & Ohio, Fort Wayne, Jackson & Saginaw, and Eel River Railroads. Travelers could transfer from one train to another there to make connections to get to their ultimate destinations. The Union Depot building was moved to the northwest corner of Union and 15th Streets and is now a residence.

Jacob Stamets moved his hotel to "The Junction" and a town grew around the railroads. Hack service was provided to the courthouse square to connect with trains. The first train passed through Auburn Junction on November 1, 1875. The Baltimore & Ohio Railroad provided excellent passenger and freight service east and west.

Within five years, three railroads were constructed through or near Auburn. The town that progress had passed by and which doubted itself was ready to start its own industrial revolution. Railroads were the only means of inter-city and interstate commerce in this era. Rivers were viable transportation only for those cities located on riverbanks. The canal system was a dismal failure. From 1870 to 1890, there was a frantic effort to build railroads to criss-cross the Midwest. Many failed. Boomtowns came and went. A viable railroad was the lifeline of a town.

Auburn's three railroads provided a means of bringing raw materials into town and then shipping finished products out to regional or national markets.

Area farmers now had a market for their livestock, grain, milk, cream, and produce. Grain elevators were built at several locations throughout Auburn—at

AUBURN JUNCTION. Three major railroads intersected at Auburn Junction—the Baltimore & Ohio Railroad, the Vandalia Railroad, and the Fort Wayne, Jackson & Saginaw Railroad. The Union Depot is in the right background. It is now located at East Fifteenth and South Union Streets.

the southeast corner of North Street and Indiana Avenue on the Fort Wayne, Jackson & Saginaw Railroad; east of the intersection of Union Street and Ensley Avenue on the Eel River Railroad; and on Wayne Street south of Ensley Avenue, which was served by a siding of the Eel River Railroad. There was also a feed mill and hatchery at the southwest corner of Union and Ninth Streets. Farmers shipped out eggs, onions, beets, fruit, and other commodities by rail.

When farmers came to Auburn to sell or ship their products, they used the proceeds to purchase items from Auburn merchants, thus creating a good local economy.

Timber and cordwood now had a market. What had been a waste product, to be laboriously cut, stacked, and burned in huge smoldering fires, became a cash crop. Industrious farmers cut cordwood to supply the railroads. Large virgin trees were felled and hauled to Auburn to sell to timber buyers, who sawed them into dimension lumber.

The most profound effect of the railroads on Auburn was industrialization. Virtually, the growth of every Auburn industry, past and present, can be traced to its proximity to one of Auburn's railroads.

While the Civil War was horrible, it did have the positive effect of linking the Midwest to the rest of the United States and providing a mindset that encouraged the movement of people from one area to another for non-farming purposes.

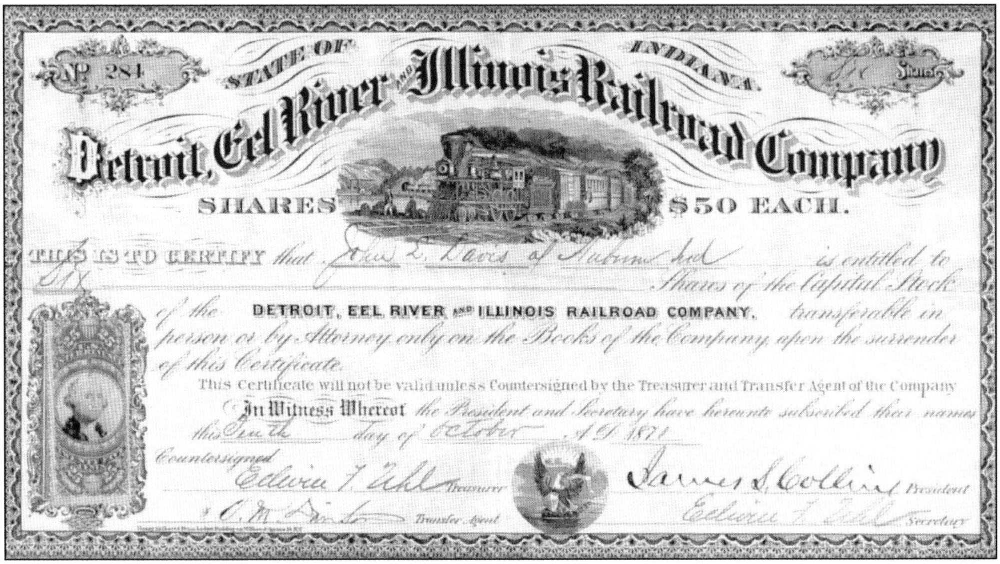

DETROIT, EEL RIVER & ILLINOIS RAILROAD COMPANY STOCK CERTIFICATE. Later known as the Vandalia, this railroad served Eckhart Carriage Company and later Auburn Automobile Company.

Several Civil War veterans migrated to Auburn after the Civil War. One of these was William H. McIntosh, who became an important educator and historian. Another was Charles Eckhart, who was to become one of Auburn's most prominent citizens.

Eckhart was born in Germantown, Pennsylvania in 1841 and began working in his father's woolen mill at the age of eight. The mill closed in 1857 due to an economic recession. He then apprenticed himself to a carriage maker. At 19 years of age, he purchased the shop of his master with unsecured notes. At the beginning of the Civil War, he sold his shop and enlisted.

After the war, Eckhart came west and worked as a carriage maker in Kendallville, Indiana. While there, he visited Waterloo and met Barbara Ellen Ashelman of Auburn, whom he married in 1866. They returned to Pennsylvania where he continued to work as a carriage maker. In 1874, they returned to Indiana and he started building carriages. The first unit was built in the parlor of the Ashleman home at 915 East Seventh Street. In 1875, he erected a modest two-story shop behind the home, measuring 18 feet by 24 feet.

Eckhart was his own chief mechanic, expert woodworker, painter, and trimmer for many years. In due course, his sons Frank and Morris went into the business and worked in all phases of it to learn all of the trades involved in carriage building.

In 1896, the sons were made partners and the carriage business turned over to them. There were many buildings enclosing over 60,000 square feet of floor space. The plant turned out from 35 to 40 vehicles a day and between 4,000 and 5,000 units annually. Over 100 men were employed.

The plant was located on the south side of Seventh Street, generally east of Iwo Street and extending east to about Dewey Street. The Vandalia Railroad ran multiple sidings into the grounds. Most raw material and finished goods were shipped in and out by rail. The Ashelman house at the southeast corner of Iwo and Seventh Streets was used as offices.

The Eckhart Carriage Company was incorporated in 1888 with Charles Eckhart, Frank E. Eckhart, Alonzo D. Northam, Nicholas Ensley, and Oliver P. Ensley as the initial board of directors. Its purposes were for "repairing and manufacturing of sleighs, buggies, carriages, and other vehicles." The Eckharts's company was to become one of the most successful carriage manufacturers and was the direct ancestor of the Auburn Automobile Company.

Many other horse-drawn vehicles were manufactured in Auburn. The Auburn Manufacturing Company was incorporated July 10, 1873 by a group of prominent Auburn businessmen for the purpose of "manufacturing hubs and spokes and such other articles manufactured of wood, entering into the structure of wagons and carriages." The initial board of directors was composed of Michael Sheets, Samuel B. Miller, and John P. Widney. The company's shares were valued at $25 each. Its capital was $25,000.

The company built the three-story building on Lincoln Street between South Jackson and South Wayne Streets and began the manufacture of wood hubs and spokes. Rough sawn logs were brought in by teams of horses and rail and were stored in the yard north of the building. The logs were sawn into dimension stock and then turned into hubs and spokes. The company later made buggy and wagon bodies and other wood components.

The Auburn Wagon and Buggy Works was located in the present Rieke Plant at 500 West Seventh Street in Auburn and was operated by a partnership known as Snyder, Mclellan, and Best. Its catalog Number 34 states its philosophy:

> On the first page of this catalog we show a cut of our factory, the most modern vehicle factory in the world. It is equipped with every modern labor saving machine that will reduce the cost of production. Before building this factory, we visited every one of the largest and best vehicle factories all over the United States, with the view of combining in our plant every advantage all the others possessed, and the result is, our factory is so constructed with reference to light, finishing and shipping of vehicles, as to keep the cost down to the lowest figure.
>
> No part of our vehicles ever travel over the same track twice. The different rough materials are received in carload lots at one end of our factory, and from there they pass through one department to another, until it goes out the other end of the factory, a finished vehicle, ready to crate and ship. We don't allow a vehicle to leave our factory until the varnish has become thoroughly hard and dry, and until the vehicle has been carefully inspected.

W.H. Kiblinger Company was organized by William H. Kiblinger in 1887. He had moved to Auburn from Williamsburg, Indiana in 1877 and established a hardware business on the north side of the square. In 1880, he built the two-story brick building at the northeast corner of Main and Seventh Streets and moved his hardware to that location.

In 1887, Kiblinger bought out the small buggy manufacturing business of I.N. Cool, located at the northeast corner of Jackson and Eighth Streets. The business grew rapidly under Kiblinger's direction and soon additional space was required. He then built two large buildings on the east side of Jackson Street between Seventh and Ninth Streets. The north building at 131 West Seventh Street still stands, but has been modified substantially. Over 4,000 vehicles were built in 1891 in these two buildings.

W.H. Kiblinger died on May 3, 1894 at the age of 45, apparently of lung cancer. The *Auburn Courier* reported that "no death that happened in Auburn for years has produced such profound earnest sorrow."

After the death of Kiblinger, W.H. McIntyre, who was then a banker, was appointed personal representative of his estate. On September 7, 1894, McIntyre, Simon C. Snyder, and their wives incorporated the W.H. Kiblinger Company with a capital of $75,000 and acquired the business assets of the Kiblinger estate.

They continued manufacturing carriages and, in 1904, acquired the assets of the Modern Buggy Company from its receiver, William H. Rakestraw, for the sum of $25,300. This included the four-story brick building at 500 West Seventh Street, built by the Auburn Wagon and Buggy Works, now owned by Rieke Corporation.

The Zimmerman Manufacturing Company was a major manufacturer of buggies, windmills, and plumbing and water supplies. The company was started by Elias Zimmerman as a sawmill in Spencerville in 1874. It began manufacturing axe handles, barrel staves, and other parts made from wood. The company moved to Auburn in the 1880s and was incorporated in 1886. The officers in 1889 were J.W. Baxter, president; Elias Zimmerman, secretary; Albert Robbins, treasurer; and Frank T. Zimmerman, superintendent.

ZIMMERMAN MANUFACTURING COMPANY. Located on North Indiana Avenue, this company manufactured a wide variety of products, including carriages, road wagons, Monarch Wind Engines, oak hubs, elm hub blanks, regulators, pumps, and tanks.

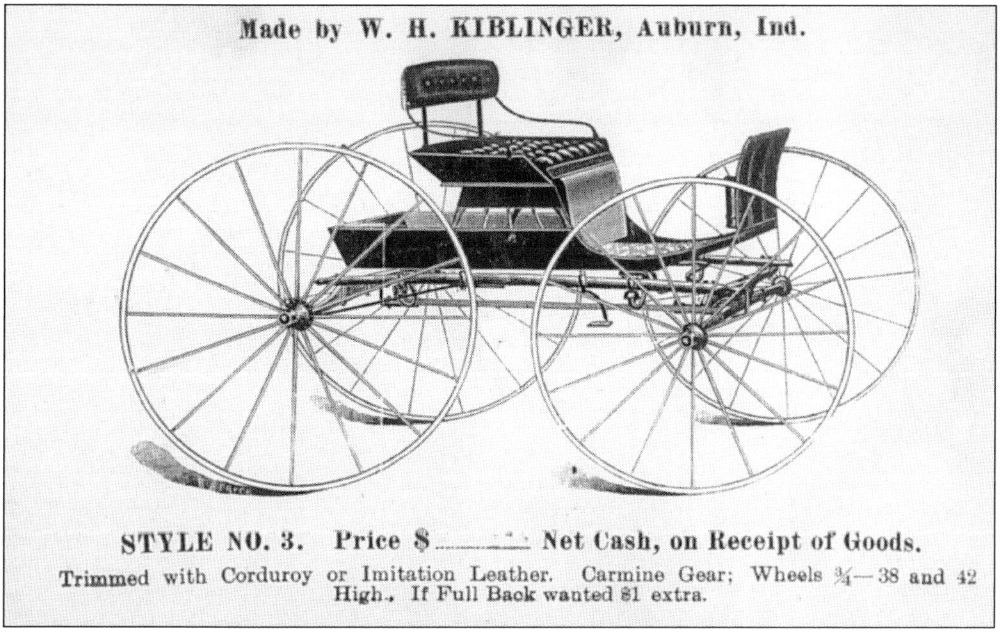

W.H. KIBLINGER BUGGY STYLE NO. 3. Buggies were offered in many different styles and configurations.

The company began manufacturing buggies in 1890 and automobiles in 1908. The company's windmills were sold under the name Monarch Wind Engine. The manufacturing facilities were located north of Fifth Street between North Indiana Avenue and the Fort Wayne, Jackson & Saginaw Railroad. Zimmerman's buggy manufacturing business continued until 1909 when it was sold to the Eckhart Carriage Company.

Other horse-drawn vehicle manufacturers in Auburn included Englebert Ashlee Wagon Shops (1885), Rockey Carriage Company (1890s), J.W. Shafer Wagon Shop (1885), Snyder Wagon Company (1880s), Specialty Buggy Company (1900), Yesbera-Rockey Carriage Company (1900), and C.B. Weaver and Company (1902).

Except for local sales, all of these companies crated their buggies and shipped them by rail. Each was located adjacent to or near one of Auburn's three rail lines. Manufacturing depended on the vast supply of hardwoods cut in this area and brought to the factories by local farmers or timber buyers. Iron was shipped in by rail and forged or cast into the metal parts needed to construct a buggy.

Many other industries were established in Auburn from 1871 to 1900. These included B. Goodman Company (1880s), which manufactured zinc cornices, window caps, and similar architectural devices painted to look like stone; Seibly and Row Broom Company (1880); Marrell Brother's Foundry (1884); Jacob Mitchell Sawmill and Hoop Factory (1885); James A. Clifton Broom Factory (1885); Auburn Church Furniture Company (1887); Auburn Broom Company (1888); Shrock and Cass and Company (1888), which manufactured wind engines, regulators, and pumps; Auburn Foundry and Machine Works (1888); Auburn Windmill Company (1889); Eagle Iron Works (1890); Office Supply Company (1891); Indiana Dimension Stock Company (1892); Kuppetz-Metcher Brewery (1895); Auburn Foundry and Machine Company (1897); and Standard Manufacturing Corporation (1899), which manufactured electric cigar lighters.

An analysis of these industries reveals certain trends. The foundries provided parts for the buggy and windmill companies. The furniture, windmill, and broom companies used raw materials of wood and broom straw which were supplied locally.

Only the zinc cornice, brewery, and electric cigar lighter companies produced consumer items. There are examples of the zinc cornices on the Culberston-Penfield-Hines House at the southwest corner of South Main and Tenth Streets. These cornices look like stone, but make a "hollow thump" when tapped. This company may have also made tombstones that look like stone, but are actually zinc.

Auburn's industrial revolution had a large impact on commercial, residential, and social life in the town. The population gradually grew from 639 in 1860, to 677 in 1870, to 1,542 in 1880, to 2,415 in 1890, and to 3,396 in 1900. More lots were platted and houses built to house the workers. Most of these were clustered around the factories. All employees walked to work and many walked home for lunch. Most of these houses were of simple, utilitarian architecture, and their sturdy construction permits them to still be very functional homes today.

The downtown area continued to expand to meet the needs of the workers for goods and services. Many of the present downtown buildings were erected during this era and still provide retail space for Auburn's downtown merchants.

Streets were not paved because there was no material suitable for such purpose other than bricks. Wood sidewalks were prevalent, although stone sidewalks were installed in some areas. Nearly all residents walked everywhere they went within the town. If they needed to go to another town, they went by rail. If they needed to go out into the country, they rented a horse and buggy from the livery stable on the east side of the square. If they were affluent enough to have their own horse and buggy, there would have been a stable on their lot. An example of a stable from the era is located at 117 East 11th Street.

There was no sewer or water system, so a pump and well and an outhouse were necessary for each house. The fuel of both choice and necessity for cooking and for warmth was still wood supplied by local farmers.

Yet, life had become more civil and genteel. Livestock no longer roamed the streets. Waterwagons kept dust down in the summer. There was increased social interaction, particularly within lodges. The Odd Fellows Lodge was organized in 1852, the Knights of Pythias in 1888, and the Masonic Lodge in 1857. All of these had ladies' auxiliaries.

Lodges provided social interaction and entertainment for members and their families. Members met at least once a week on an established night. Ladies met on another night. Dinners were frequently attended by the whole family.

Lodges became quite prosperous and frequently built their own buildings. An example is the Odd Fellows Building on the north side of the square. It contained retail store front space on the ground floor, space for offices for attorneys, doctors, and insurance agents on the second floor, and lodge rooms on the third floor. The lodge rooms included a large open space with "stations," a dining room area, and frequently a room for pool tables and card playing. Dues from the members and income from the rental of the ground and second floor spaces provided funds to pay for and maintain the building.

The GAR became a prominent organization of Civil War veterans. The veterans were revered as heroes and frequently appeared in parades in unison, in uniform, marching to the beat of a fife and drum corps. Like a lodge, the GAR also had a social aspect for the benefit of the veterans and their families.

The Second Battalion of the 3rd Infantry of the Indiana National Guard was headquartered at Auburn under the command of Captain—later Major—Aubrey L. Kuhlman. A two-story armory was built at the northeast corner of Cedar and East Seventh Streets. The post office was on the ground floor and the Armory rooms were on the second floor. The building still stands without the second floor.

The Armory was the location of many social events such as the Auburn Military Board Trust Annual Ball held May 17, 1893. The dances included "May Pole, Waltz, Lanciers, Duchess, Quadrille, Schotlishche, Polka, York and Grand

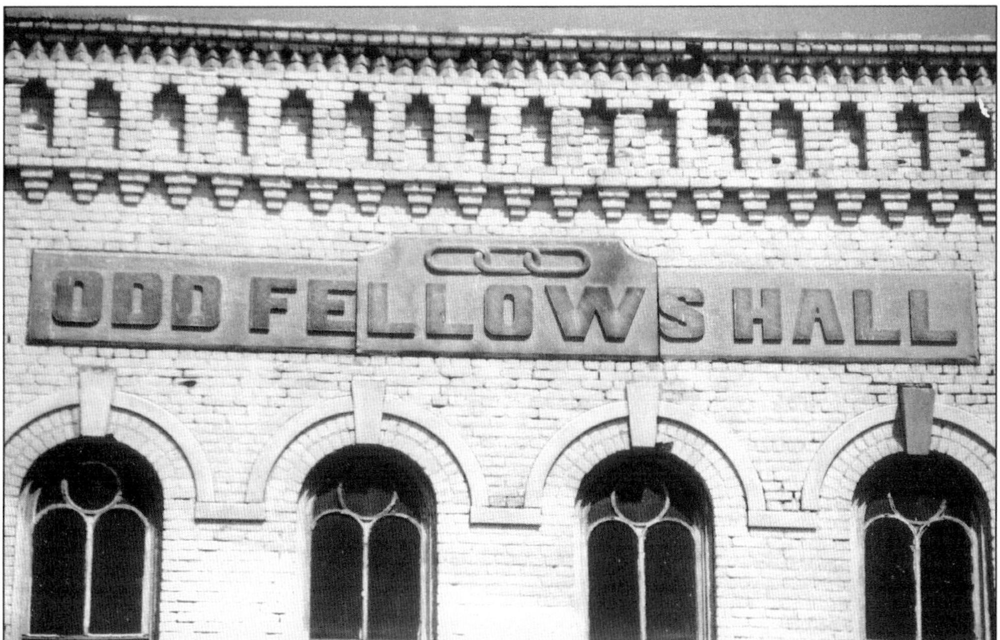

ODD FELLOWS HALL. The three-story building on the north side of the square provided a handsome home for this popular lodge. It had retail space on the ground floor, office space on the second floor, and lodge rooms on the third floor.

CENTRAL UNION TELEPHONE COMPANY. *This 1909 postcard encouraged the use of long distance over the Christmas holiday.*

March." The Auburn Dancing Club held a Select Ball and Reception at the Armory on December 28, 1893, with additional dances including the "Newport, Virginia Reel, and Ladies Choice Quadrille."

Churches and church buildings continued to grow and to be established in Auburn. The Methodists moved their building from the northwest corner of East Seventh and Cedar Streets to the southeast corner of North Van Buren and West Sixth Streets in 1874. In 1890, the frame church was moved to the McKinney Harrison School grounds and a magnificent brick edifice was built between West Seventh and West Sixth Streets, east of North Van Buren Street.

The Baptist church was built at the northwest corner of North Jackson and West Sixth Streets in 1873. The Presbyterian church built a handsome new building in 1876 at the southeast corner of South Jackson and West 12th Streets.

Saint Marks Lutheran Church was built at the southeast corner of South Jackson and Ninth Streets in 1875. The Catholic church was established in 1881 and a church built at the northeast corner of North Indiana and West Fifth Streets in 1889.

Two fine elementary schools were built in Auburn during this era. The Riley School was located at the northeast corner of North Van Buren and First Streets. The DeSoto School was located between Cleveland and Baxter Streets, south of Seventh Street. Both were razed many years ago and the sites are now neighborhood parks.

Communication improved in 1876 when Western Union initiated telegraph service with lines along the Fort Wayne, Jackson & Saginaw Railroad, followed by Indiana Postal Telegraph in 1882 and Bankers and Merchants Telegraph Company in 1884.

Much commercial business was conducted via telegraphic messages, which were often in code words. For example, a buggy catalog may have contained a code word for each model such as "HIP" for a "Model 23 with double seats and kerosene lights." By using one simple word, eight words were omitted from the message. Since charges were on a "per word" basis, the use of code words saved considerable money.

Telephone service was initiated in Auburn in 1886 when John L. Davis connected his Pioneer Hardware in Auburn with his Pioneer Hardware in Garrett. The connection was a line for his private use, but he sometimes permitted others to communicate between the two towns.

In 1893, the Central Union Telephone Company began service followed by the Home Telephone Company in 1896. These two telephone companies were competitors, but their lines were not connected with each other. A subscriber to one service could only call another subscriber of that company. Most merchants had both telephones—Home and Central Union. In 1919, the Home Company sold its lines to Central Union, which became a part of the Bell System in 1920.

As industrialization continued, the once vast supply of local wood for fuel dwindled. Coal was available by rail, but was expensive compared to wood. Auburn was hungry for an alternative source of fuel. It was indeed fortuitous that natural gas was discovered in Auburn in 1887. The Auburn Mining Company was incorporated on March 14, 1887 by a number of prominent Auburn businessmen "to bore for water, oil, and natural gas and to lay pipes through cities and towns to distribute same." The articles of incorporation were soon amended on July 8, 1889 to include the power to "construct and maintain and operate electric light works and selling electric light and power." Gas production continued for many years and soon became the fuel of choice for industry. Natural gas was also used for lighting homes and factories and for street lights. The Natural Gas Addition was platted east of Cedar Creek between East Seventh and East 11th Streets.

A gas line was run to the top of the courthouse tower where a large torch light flame burned night and day at a height of 115 feet! When the supplies of natural gas waned, the DeKalb County Fuel, Light, and Power Company was formed in 1906 to manufacture gas from coke shipped in by rail to Auburn Junction.

The Auburn town board entered into a lease for an Ahrens Steam Fire Engine on July 6, 1885. The Hoosier Boys Fire Company was organized November 9, 1885 to provide the town with fire protection.

There were 30 fire cisterns constructed in Auburn, which were kept full by springs and ground water. At the sound of the fire bell, the team of horses was hitched to the steam fire engine. A small fire was kept going constantly in the engine, which was fed and stoked while the engine was on its way to the fire. By the time the engine arrived, steam was up to sufficient pressure to pump water from the nearest cistern into the fire. Alarm boxes were installed in 1891 and water hydrants were first used in 1898.

The development of the automobile in Auburn closely paralleled the development of working, successful automobiles in the United States. While George Selden was granted a patent for a "motorcar" in 1877, he did not actually build an automobile until he was entwined in litigation with Henry Ford, who fought the validity of the Selden patent.

There are two well-documented examples of early automobiles that were built within an 80-mile radius of Auburn. L. Scott Bailey, the respected former editor of *Automobile Quarterly*, declared in a 1960 article that the Lambert built by John W. Lambert in 1891 at Ohio City, Ohio was the first practical, working automobile built in the United States. And there is no dispute that Elwood Haynes operated his first automobile on the Pumpkinvine Pike near Kokomo, Indiana on July 4, 1894. His run was reported in the local newspaper the following day.

For many years, documentation has been sought as to the first car built in Auburn. An intriguing entry in the November 1895 issue of *The Horseless Age* magazine indicated that R.W. Guilford (Russell Wellington Guilford) of Auburn, Indiana entered the first automobile race in the United States sponsored by the *Chicago Herald Times* in 1895. The race was to be run in Chicago on Labor Day, 1895. Over 80 cars were entered. However, because many were unable to finish their cars in time, the race was postponed until November 2, 1895. On that date, only two cars arrived and the race was again postponed to Thanksgiving Day, November 28, 1895.

One would assume that if Guilford entered the *Chicago Herald Times* race in June 1895 (when entries were due), he had built a car by then. The *Auburn Courier* documented his early efforts on October 31, 1895:

> The *Chicago Times Herald* has arranged for a race of the new style of road wagons, the ones that are to be run by steam, electricity, etc., or in any way without horses. It is to take place on Saturday of this week. The start is to be made from near the Midway in Jackson Park, and the route is along the west side of the city and up north a little past Waukegan, then to Waukegan so on back through the towns on the lake shore to Lincoln Park in the City of Chicago. The distance traveled is 100 miles. Entries have been made by people from all parts of the country, including one by our fellow townsman, R.W. Guilford. It is a poor day when Auburn gets left out. It is believed a vast audience will witness the start, and that from this beginning will date the use of horseless vehicles. Between this plan and the trolley cars and steam plows it looks as if the noblest of all animals would be put into the background.

The paper reported again on November 7, 1895:

> Last Wednesday, a queer craft, as sailors would say, appeared on our streets. It was Rus Guilford's steam wagon. He has been making a new steam engine for some time, and having finished it concluded to attach

RUSSELL W. GUILFORD AUTOMOBILE. This large, six-cylinder automobile was built by Russell W. Guilford and is shown on Eighth Street adjacent the W.H. Kiblinger factory.

> it to a wagon and make a "Motocycle." So, having it all ready for trial, he came up to town that day, and ran about on several streets. It worked very well, we are told, though we did not see it and he expects to go on and improve it still more. He has entered it for the great motocycle race that is to take place at Chicago on Saturday of this week.
>
> . . . the latest of the extraordinary things that Auburn gets is the selection of W.H. McIntyre of the Kiblinger Carriage Factory as one of the umpires or judges in the great motocycle contest in Chicago Saturday. This is the first ever held in the world, which gives it additional prominence. Mr. McIntyre has accepted and has already gone to the city.

This is very reliable historical documentation that Guilford built a working car and operated it on the streets of Auburn as early as October 30, 1895.

After being postponed twice, the *Chicago Herald Times* race was finally run on November 28, 1895. Unfortunately, a huge snowstorm struck Chicago and only six cars were able to get there. Frank Duryea was the winner of the 55-mile race and collected the $2,000 first prize. The Duryea Brothers became pioneers in the manufacturing of automobiles, which was shortened due to the weather conditions.

The sole entry from Indiana that actually appeared in Chicago was Haynes-Apperson from Kokomo. This vehicle failed to start the race, however, because of an accident that occurred shortly before the beginning of the race.

W.H. McIntyre and P.J. Lockwood of Auburn were there. The *Auburn Courier* reported the following on December 5, 1895:

> W.H. McIntyre was at Chicago Thursday, as he was one of the injuries in the Motocycle race. The snow was so deep up there that teams could hardly get about, yet the Motocycles, some of them, made the run of sixty or seventy miles. P.J. Lockwood was up there with him.

McIntyre was apparently assigned as referee either to one of the cars that did not appear at the starting line or to one of the cars that had an accident. It is also possible that he could have been a passenger in the Haynes-Apperson entry.

Auburn automotive pioneers had a significant part in the 1895 *Chicago Times-Herald* race, which many historians believe provided the impetus for the development of the automobile industry in the United States. It is known that Guilford later worked for W.H. McIntyre. There are photographs of one of his early cars adjacent to the Kiblinger/McIntyre Factory between Seventh and Eighth Streets on the east side of South Jackson Street (now Auburn House Restaurant).

Obviously, Guilford's car could have been built and operated earlier, but not documented or reported. The *Auburn Courier* reports provide reliable contemporary documentation that the earliest car built in Auburn was operated as early as October 30, 1895. Russell Guilford apparently built his own steam engine in his bicycle shop. He was known to be an accomplished machinist.

In the meantime, the skilled machinists brought to Garrett by the Baltimore & Ohio Railroad were building steam and gasoline engines. The Garrett Engine Boiler and Machine Works was incorporated on January 31, 1895 to build gas and steam engines. The Model Gas Engine Company was organized October 11, 1900. Incorporators included Edward A. Myers, who had been counsel for the Garrett Company, and Albert Robbins, a banker who was treasurer of the Zimmerman Manufacturing Company that made buggies and windmills.

At the end of the nineteenth century, Auburn was a busy, prosperous town with a good infrastructure in place or under construction. Its buggy, wagon, and windmill factories were in full operation. Many trains stopped at Auburn each day to load and unload passengers and freight from distant points.

The nation and Auburn were on the verge of the "automobile revolution." Auburn was ready.

AUBURN—CITY OF HONEST ENDEAVOR. This license plate topper was cast in aluminum.

5. Vision, Guts, and Perseverance: The Golden Era of Automobiles (1900–1915)

Two strawberry ice-cream sodas, yes sir, Yes, sir. There are a hundred and twenty-five horses in Grover's Corners this minute I'm talking to you. State Inspector was in here yesterday. And now they're bringing in these auto-mo-biles, the best thing to do is to just stay home. Why, I can remember when a dog could go to sleep all day in the middle of Main Street and nothing come along to disturb him.

~Thornton Wilder, *Our Town*

This era had to be Auburn's most exciting! If one could go back in history in a time capsule, he would see many interesting developments in the history of our town during this era.

Auburn became a city under Indiana law in 1900. Multiple car and truck companies came and went. A new courthouse, library, and city park were built. A future vice president of the United States announced his candidacy for the presidency on our square. Many fine homes were built along our tree-lined streets. It was a good time to live in Auburn. It is the heritage that we preserve and celebrate in the museums of Auburn.

Auburn became a city on March 26, 1900. The reasons why the change was made from an incorporated *town* to an incorporated *city* are now obscure, but it likely was a result of the need to finance the public utilities that were being installed. Some Indiana towns comparable to the size of Auburn have continued as towns to this day. On March 5, 1900, John C. Henry presented a petition to the Auburn Town Board for Auburn to become a city. The petition was signed by 322 registered voters, which constituted just over one-third of the registered voters at the time.

The primary difference between a town and a city is that a town is governed by a town board comprised of three to five members, which is both the legislative and administrative body. A city has a city council, which is the legislative body, and a mayor, who is the administrator. The city form of government has served Auburn well. The city has had healthy growth in its more than 100 years of existence.

Don A. Garwood, Auburn's first mayor, was born March 9, 1858 in Cassopolis, Michigan. He graduated from the University of Michigan in 1881. He immediately moved to Waterloo, Indiana and entered the law office of Best and McClellan where he read and studied the law. He was admitted to the bar in 1883 and, upon the retirement of Attorney Best, became a partner with Attorney McClellan under the firm name of McClellan and Garwood.

Garwood was active in many civic and fraternal organizations. He was on the initial board of directors of the Auburn Improvement Association, formed in 1895, and the Auburn Commercial Club, organized in 1903. He was a member of Waterloo City Lodge Number 307, Free and Accepted Masons, and was Worshipful Master of DeKalb Lodge Number 214, Free and Accepted Masons. Garwood and his wife Jennie McClellan Garwood resided at 207 South Van Buren Street in Auburn.

Donald A. Garwood was president of the Auburn Town Board prior to his election as mayor on May 1, 1900. A Republican, he defeated his opponent Thomas A. Sprott by just 364 to 362. The first clerk was Charles B. Weaver (R). The first treasurer was David A. Hodge (R). The new city was divided into three districts with two councilmen for each district: John Zimmerman (R) and Milen E. Garrett (R), First District; Howard McCord (R) and John B. Relope (D), Second District; and Perry A. Mukon (D) and Eli T. Cochran (D), Third District.

Auburn was a dynamic, growing city in 1900. It was served by three railroads—the Vandalia, the Fort Wayne & Jackson, and the Baltimore & Ohio. The economy was good; industry was booming.

AUBURN AUTOMOBILE COMPANY ASSEMBLY LINE. This photograph was taken c. 1910. Frames were mounted on dollies, which could be pushed through the assembly area.

However, there was much to be done.

There were no paved streets, no water system, and no sewer system, plus the electric system was primitive and privately owned. The streets were made of dirt with little, if any, gravel. The only sidewalks were in the downtown area and were made of sawn timber or slabs of stone. Water was supplied by private wells with hand pumps. Sewage was via outhouses at every residence and business. There was a public privy on the southeast corner of the square, adjacent to the jail. The town pump was located on the north side of the square. Electricity was starting to come into use on a limited basis.

The Auburn Commercial Club was organized on February 14, 1903. The name of the organization was changed in 1929 to the Chamber of Commerce of Auburn, Indiana. In 1957, the corporate structure was reorganized and the name was again changed to the Auburn Chamber of Commerce, Inc.

The 1903 organization may have been a successor, at least in function, to the Auburn Improvement Association, which had been incorporated December 5, 1895 "to use its influence and expand its assets to encourage manufacturing and other industrial companies and enterprises to locate in the town of Auburn, Indiana."

The decade beginning in 1900 was the golden era of industrial development in DeKalb County. Many of the present industries can trace their roots to this era, directly or indirectly. The Auburn Commercial Club was largely responsible for this growth. The club was quick to recruit industry. When the Model Gas Engine Company failed, the Auburn Commercial Club bought the facility and leased it to the fledgling Auburn Automobile Company. When Theodore Rieke was looking for a site to relocate his machine shop from Chicago, the Auburn Commercial Club built a new building for the company at the southwest corner of 15th and Hazel Streets. The foresight of the Auburn Chamber of Commerce and its predecessors has proven to be invaluable to the healthy growth of the city and county.

The first decade of the twentieth century was wide open to entrepreneurship and capitalism. The era provided free enterprise in its nearly perfect form. There was virtually no government regulation. There was no income tax. There was no sales tax. The only tax was a property tax that was used to provide "bare bones" government. Transportation and communication were good. Raw materials were available. The economy was good. National and regional markets could be developed quite easily.

There was a great demand for better transportation, particularly on a local basis. Railroads provided excellent inter-city and interstate transportation, but one could only travel where the tracks went and when the timetables allowed.

Farmers still had to hitch up their teams of horses to come to town with their grain or to shop. Within towns and cities, one had to walk, keep a horse and buggy in a stable near the house, or hire a horse and buggy from a livery stable. As towns and cities grew, there was a demand for intra-city transportation. Trolley lines were established in many large cities, but trolleys had the same problems as the railroads—one could go only where the tracks and wires went.

It was within this context that Auburn's automobile industry originated and flourished. Even with the best of conditions, it was not easy to start an automobile company. It still took a deep vision, a certain amount of "guts," and certainly perseverance.

It also took the convergence of several factors—capital to finance the investment in buildings, equipment, and raw materials; skilled workers to provide the labor to build the product; and an entrepreneur to provide the vision, guts, and perseverance to manage and nourish the company through its early stages and to maintain its success. Within any company, there must be the skills to engineer and build the product and the skills to sell it to the public.

Four major companies evolved within Auburn—Auburn Automobile Company, Model Gas Engine Company, W.H. Kiblinger (later W.H. McIntyre Company), and Zimmerman Manufacturing Company. Of these four, only the Model Gas Engine Company was entirely new. The others were established manufacturers of buggies and also windmills in the case of Zimmerman Manufacturing Company. The established companies already had manufacturing facilities and a sales method or organization in place. They merely adapted to a new product.

Who was first? The answer to that question is lost to the ages. Russell W. Guilford is documented to have operated his steam-powered motocycle on the streets of Auburn as early as October 30, 1895. He operated a bicycle shop in the 200 block of East Ninth Street, but was probably involved with W.H. McIntyre, who was the owner of W.H. Kiblinger Company. It is certainly logical and likely that they continued their experimentation, but probably did not actually manufacture gasoline-powered automobiles until 1907 under the Kiblinger name.

There is folklore that Charles Eckhart first rode in an automobile in 1900 when he was running for governor of Indiana on the Prohibition ticket. Eckhart's sons Frank and Morris then ordered a curved-dash Oldsmobile. Charles Eckhart and his sons were the owners of the Eckhart Carriage Company, founded in 1874, and later were the founders of the Auburn Automobile Company.

Morris and Frank Eckhart realized that their Oldsmobile was rather primitive and sought a Winton, like the one driven by a local doctor. Unable to purchase one, they obtained a Rutenber engine at Logansport, Indiana and began experimenting. It is likely that the first production car was built by the Eckharts in late 1902. They may have called the first cars "Eckharts" rather than "Auburns." The earliest Auburn known to exist is a 1904 model in the Auburn Cord Duesenberg Museum collection.

Is there other evidence? The earliest known photograph of an Auburn is of a 1902. The earliest brochure was published in 1903. The earliest advertisement located to date is a small ad in *The Automobile* dated June 27, 1903. In the 1903 program of the Buffalo, New York Automobile Show, there is a reference to an entry in the show by "Eckhart."

The Auburn Automobile Company exhibited a car at the Chicago Automobile Show February 14–21, 1903. A brief article in *Cycle and Automobile Trade Journal*, dated March 1, 1903, describes "The Auburn Gasoline Automobile" as follows:

The Auburn Automobile Company of Auburn, Ind., one of the later arrivals in the field, showed for the first time their gasoline toneau car. The motor is of the four-cycle type and is cooled by forced circulation through a copper pipe radiator, which is hung in front beneath the frame. A float feed carburetor is used and ignition is by jump spark. The transmission is by a sun and planet gear for the slow forward speed and the reverse and by direct clutch connection for the high speed. The transmission gear and motor are mounted upon a solid frame entirely independent of the carriage frame.

The wheels are of the artillery type and spokes and rims are of second-growth hickory. They are 28 inches in diameter and fitted with 3 inch clincher tires. The springs are oil tempered and are graded for the load. Radius rods are dispensed with by connecting back springs with the frame and providing adjustment at the forward end. The axles are modular. The rear one is divided and fitted with a Brown-Life differential.

The body is well made and handsomely finished. Spring cushions, well filled with hair make comfortable seating. Leather is used as a covering. The body is painted maroon with black moldings and the gear is finished in carmine.

The motor is started with a removable crank and its speed is controlled by throttling the mixture and timing spark. The forward speeds are

AUBURN AUTOMOBILE COMPANY. New Auburns, c. 1912, are being prepared for shipment on the factory grounds.

AUBURN AUTOMOBILE COMPANY. The original buildings were adjacent to the Vandalia Railroad tracks and Ensley Avenue.

> obtained by a lever at the right of the operator and the reverse by a foot lever. Band brakes acting on the transmission and on the rear axle are operated by a foot lever. The body can be removed by taking out four nuts and detaching spark timer and switch wires. All adjustments of the motor and transmission can be made without detaching any other parts.

The Auburn Automobile Company was not incorporated until August 22, 1903. It is possible that an automobile was built by the Eckhart Carriage Company or the Eckhart brothers before that date, but documented historical facts indicate that the first Auburn was built in 1902.

In later years, the advertising agency of Auburn Automobile Company apparently thought that "Established 1900" sounded and looked better than "Established 1902." A 1919 advertisement in *Motor* magazine states, "Automobile Engineers for Twenty Years." This would indicate that Auburn Automobile Company started in 1899! This was an era when competition was keen and it was probably thought desirable to advertise one's longevity in the manufacturing of automobiles. Also, after a group of Chicago investors had purchased the company, the corporate memory of the founding Eckharts was no longer present.

Was it really 1900? Historical documentation indicates otherwise. Original Auburn Automobile Company invoices dated between 1910 and 1918 state "Established 1902!" It stands to reason that if the company were really founded in 1900, this date would have been claimed in 1910—just ten years later.

Whatever the date was, it can be said that the Auburn was the first car manufactured on a production basis. The second marquee to go into production was the "Model." The Model Gas Engine Company was organized in 1900. After its bankruptcy in 1904, the principals organized the Model Gas Engine Works and purchased the assets of the former company. The company had been organized to manufacture gasoline engines, both stationary and mobile. The first Model automobile was probably built in 1903. The first cars were 12-horsepower, 2-cylinder touring cars with a removable tonneau. A 16-horsepower engine was offered later.

A unique feature of the Model was that the entire body of the car was hinged at the back so it could be tipped for access to the engine and other mechanical parts, in a manner similar to the way the cabs of today's modern cabover trucks are tilted forward for servicing.

The company manufactured an extensive array of engines, clutches, and transmissions—virtually complete power and drive units—which could be bolted into automobiles by the many small, independent manufacturers that were prolific throughout the county.

In 1906, the company moved to Peru, Indiana. Its buildings south of the intersection of South Main and Ensley Streets in Auburn were purchased by the Auburn Commercial Club and leased to the Auburn Automobile Company.

After the move to Peru, the company was divided into the Model Gas Engine Works and the Model Automobile Company in 1907. The following year, the automobile company was re-christened the Great-Western Automobile Company and production continued in Peru under that name until 1914. Great-Western also produced a car called the Izzer in 1913.

The Model Gas Engine Works was sold to Pittsburgh interests in 1912 and renamed the Pittsburgh Model Engine Company. In 1915, this company was sold to the Standard Automobile Company of Butler, Pennsylvania, which built the Standard Automobile from 1914 to 1923.

There were two types of automobiles in this era—those with pneumatic tires, and high wheelers. Both Auburn and Model had pneumatic tires and were best suited to intra-city or town driving where the streets were presumably better than their rural counterparts.

High wheel vehicles had buggy-type wheels, which made the vehicle stand higher and thus be better suited to muddy, rutted rural roads. The Kiblinger/McIntyre and Zimmerman cars started out as high wheelers, but as road improvements evolved, the company changed to the lower pneumatic tire configuration.

High wheelers were generally more primitive and simple in their construction. Some were literally horseless carriages: a buggy equipped with an engine and a tiller or steering wheel. Their one- or two-cylinder engines were usually air-cooled and located directly under the seat. Conversely, the more sophisticated pneumatic tire vehicles, such as the Auburn and the Model, were water cooled with a radiator.

The evolution of the automobile companies in Auburn was a microcosm of the automobile industry as a whole across the United States. The W.H. Kiblinger Company was founded by W.H. Kiblinger in 1887 to manufacture buggies. After Kiblinger's death in 1894, W.H. McIntyre and S.C. Snyder purchased the assets of the company and incorporated. McIntyre purchased Snyder's interest in 1901.

McIntyre began experimenting with automobiles as early as 1895. He constructed several cars that may have been among the first operated in DeKalb County.

In 1906, the company decided to manufacture motor vehicles commercially. Its prototypes were completed by February 14, 1907, when the *Auburn Weekly Courier* reported, "The W.H. Kiblinger Company had a photograph taken last evening, showing the machine in different positions. They have orders booked ahead on this machine to crowd their capacity for a month at least, although they have done nothing in the way of soliciting business."

The Kiblinger was a high wheel vehicle, which sold for as little as $250. The first models were the ultimate in simplicity, literally a buggy with an engine and tiller. The Kiblinger was well received and sales were soon brisk.

In January 1907, the company issued $75,000 in preferred stock, which was sold locally. The proceeds were used to purchase the plant of the Auburn Wagon and Buggy Works at 500 West Seventh Street. At that time, assets of the company were in excess of $3 million.

Within a year, the company had acquired the building on Lincoln Street between South Wayne and Van Buren Streets and named it Plant No. 3. In 1908, a large electric motor was installed in the plant with power supplied from the lines of the Toledo and Chicago Interurban Company, which had recently installed its tracks down the middle of Ensley Avenue.

A total of 400 men were employed with 167 of them at Plant No. 3. Two shifts worked six days per week. The night men worked 62.5 hours per week and the day men worked 60 hours per week. This was a period of economic recession that had resulted in the closing of the Baltimore and Ohio Shops at Garrett. Many Garrett men worked at Kiblinger and used the Interurban for commuting.

On April 23, 1908, the *Auburn Weekly Courier* stated the following:

> It was only a little over two years ago that [the Kiblinger Motor Buggy] was offered to the trade. Now it is sought after everywhere and, at times, it is difficult to keep up with the orders. . . . It is because of their excellence and the fact that they are sold within the reach of many who would not care to invest so much money in the high priced machines.

McIntyre, the entrepreneur, had recognized and satisfied an important facet of the market for an inexpensive but durable, simple, high wheeled vehicle. In 1908, a lawsuit was filed by the Success Motor Buggy Company alleging patent infringement. In December 1908, a decree of the DeKalb Circuit Court changed the name of the company to W.H. McIntyre Company.

McINTYRE AUTOMOBILES, c. 1910. The McIntyre factory was at the southeast corner of Jackson and Seventh Streets. The three automobiles on the left have hoods and a crank in front and probably have four-cylinder engines. The three on the right probably have two-cylinder engines under the seats. The driver of the fourth car from the left is W.H. McIntyre.

The W.H. McIntyre Company continued to build horse-drawn vehicles, but the endeavor was quickly being replaced by the ever-increasing demand for automobiles. The 1908–1909 McIntyre models continued to be high wheelers, but the car soon became much more sophisticated with pneumatic tires and four-cylinder then six-cylinder engines. W.H. McIntyre built a half-mile-long track south of Auburn for testing automobiles. The frequent testing of automobiles on the streets of Auburn had created a hazard. Car races were held at the track for some time.

A line of trucks ranging in capacity to 5 tons was introduced. These were massive machines that would carry substantial loads. In September 1912, the *Auburn Courier* reported the following:

> The McIntyre truck made for G.W. Moor, the Auburn Junction drayman, was on dress parade today. It is surely a well-built nicely painted, attractive appearing truck and seemed big enough to move a whole freight house or a good sized residence and then some. The truck is the modern manner of delivery and the manufacturing of motor delivering wagons is in its infancy.

McIntyre licensed its car for manufacture in Canada under the name McIntyre Tudhope. McIntyre also helped launch the cyclecar craze in 1912 with the Imp. In 1911, the company purchased the assets of the impressively named "Motor

Car Company of America" and used its designs and engineering to build a large six-cylinder car called the McIntyre Special.

With five large plants in Auburn, the W.H. McIntyre Company enjoyed phenomenal success for several years. With vehicles ranging from horse-drawn carriages to cyclecars to trucks to large, luxurious automobiles, the company produced the largest range of vehicles of any company in Auburn.

W.H. McIntyre was a visionary who recognized and appreciated the potential of many different fields of endeavor. His experience with the use of electrical power in his plant enabled him to establish the electric and water utilities in Butler, Waterloo, and Garrett. He was also instrumental in the exploration for and development of natural gas in Auburn.

McIntyre was very generous to the City of Auburn and was active in many civic causes and organizations He was president of the National Carriage Builder's Association in 1911, quite a feat for the owner of a large automobile manufacturing company. McIntyre was also personally popular among the people of Auburn.

It was a sad day in August 1915 when the W.H. McIntyre Company was forced into bankruptcy by the Northern National Bank of Toledo, Ohio and the Hamilton National Bank of Fort Wayne. The reasons for the failure of this once-vital company are now obscure, but it was a fate met by many automobile

MCINTYRE TRUCK. This striking photograph was taken at the intersection of West Eighth and South Jackson Streets. The 26 people illustrated the capacity of the large truck. W.H. McIntyre stands in front of the truck.

companies in this era. The assets of the company were purchased by the DeKalb Manufacturing Company.

W.H. McIntyre was personally devastated by the failure of his company. His sons John and Harry were later involved in auto-related fields and were also very successful. W.H. McIntyre, despite his later financial failures, should be remembered as one of the most outstanding citizens who ever lived in DeKalb County.

The Zimmerman Manufacturing Company was established in Spencerville in 1874 and moved to Auburn in the 1880s. The company manufactured an extensive line of windmills and horse-drawn vehicles.

In 1907, the company first manufactured a single-seat runabout automobile with solid rubber tires and a two-cylinder engine. In 1909, the line was expanded to a four-cylinder standard car with 30-inch by 3-inch pneumatic tires. A six-cylinder car was added in 1911, which was marketed under both the Zimmerman and deSoto names. It was, however, actually manufactured by the Auburn Automobile Company in the Zimmerman plant pursuant to a lease or contract. In 1915, production with the Zimmerman name was discontinued and the plant on North Indiana Avenue in Auburn was leased to the Auburn Automobile Company for the production of the Union automobile.

Frank T. Zimmerman died in 1910. Elias Zimmerman retired from active participation in the company in 1910 at the age of 80 and died in 1914. The company continued to manufacture buggies until 1914 when the buggy business was consolidated with Eckhart. Both names were used by Eckhart until 1918.

Other cars built in Auburn included the Black, DeKalb, deSoto, Handy Wagon, Imp, King, McDowell, and Union.

The Black was marketed widely by mail order from 1908 to 1910 by the Black Manufacturing Company of Chicago. Catalogs for the car indicate that orders would be "shipped F.O.B. our plant in Auburn, Indiana." In fact, the car was built by the W.H. McIntyre Company. A comparison of contemporary Black and McIntyre catalogues shows that the cars were nearly identical. The Black Manufacturing Company was primarily a marketing organization and probably built few, if any, cars itself. The company was greatly encouraged by $50,000 in orders obtained at the Iowa State Fair. The high wheeler it offered was particularly suitable for farmers. The company had previously marketed the Chicago Motor Buggy.

In 1909, Black Manufacturing Company purchased the Aurora Motor Works, a manufacturer of automobile components. In the same year it joined forces with the Crow Motor Car Company of Elkhart, Indiana, to produce the Black Crow, a four-cylinder car built in 1909 and 1910. In 1910, Crow canceled the contract and began selling the same car under the name Crow-Elkhart.

The DeKalb Manufacturing Company was incorporated August 30, 1915, with capital of $150,000 for the purpose of the "manufacture and sale of vehicles especially motor driven vehicles, and other lines, identical thereto, and profitable, in connection therewith." The company was formed by the Vesey Family of Fort

Wayne with William L. Vesey, Dick M. Vesey, William J. Vesey Jr., Allen J. Vesey, and David L. Vesey as incorporators.

The new company was formed to take over the assets of the bankrupt W.H. McIntyre Company. The company offered two models—the DeKalb Sr., which was a six-cylinder car selling for $1,050, and the DeKalb Jr., selling for $690. Both were assembled cars and little manufacturing was done. It is believed that they were in production for less than two years. None are known to have survived.

Officers of the company were E.F. Yarian, president; C.H. Worden, vice president; R.N. Poole, treasurer; J.D. Casey, general manager; and Harry McIntyre, purchasing agent, the latter two having been key executives of the W.H. McIntyre Company.

The deSoto Motor Car Company was incorporated October 30, 1912, with a capital of $12,000 by I.M. Field of Auburn; Hayes Fry and Glen Fry of Iowa City, Iowa; and V. VanSickle and H.J. Clark of Des Moines, Iowa. The company was in fact a subsidiary of the Zimmerman Manufacturing Company. Its cars were a bit larger and more luxurious than its Zimmerman counterparts. The six-cylinder deSoto sold at $285, a price that included electric lights and a compressed air starter.

In 1914, the company joined the cyclecar craze and introduced a two-cylinder, 10-horsepower cyclecar with tandem seats. It was more sophisticated than most cyclecars. The cyclecar was the original economy car. As its name suggests, it was like a motorcycle with four wheels. Passengers were seated tandem, one in front of the other. The Large Six Line was also continued in 1914.

Plans for 1915 provided that the cyclecar would be renamed the Motorette, and production would be moved to Fort Wayne. The Zimmerman family patriarch, Elias Zimmerman, died in 1914. His son, John Zimmerman, decided not to continue the deSoto line, and it was dropped for 1915 production.

No examples of deSoto are known to exist. The name was sometimes written as "DeSoto" and "DeSota," but the company preferred "deSoto" in its own publications. It had no connection with the DeSoto subsequently manufactured by the Chrysler Corporation.

The Handy Wagon was built in Auburn from 1912 to 1915 by the Auburn Motor Chassis Company. It was an inexpensive high wheeler, but could be had with pneumatic tires. It was probably a continuation of the McIntyre High Wheeler line after the McIntyre cars and trucks went to pneumatic tires and larger engines. Its catalog boldly stated:

> The Handy Wagon is actually 4 cars in 1 at half the price of 1 . . . never in the history of automobile manufacturing has such a remarkable car been offered . . . the Handy Wagon represents the biggest advance in automobile construction ever offered to the buying public. Imagine, if you can, a vehicle with which you can make a quick drive from one end of the city to the other or over the farm overseeing every bit of work that is being done on any particular section, and the next minute start over a pleasure jaunt over hill and dale . . . The Handy Wagon is

made for all purposes—for pleasures, duties and emergencies that present themselves.

The vehicle was versatile in that the rear seat could be removed to turn it into a pickup truck. It was one of the last high wheel vehicles manufactured and was popular in rural areas with poor roads. The price for "four cars complete in one" was only $487.50 by mail F.O.B. Auburn.

The Imp cyclecar was one of the more unusual cars built in Auburn. In the period from 1912 to 1915, a cyclecar fad swept the country. W.H. McIntyre was quick to capitalize on the new concept. He brought William B. Stout to Auburn to engineer and design the new car, which was low and narrow. Imp advertised that it could be driven through a garden gate and stored on the front porch. It had a V2, 15-horsepower, air-cooled engine, friction transmission, belt drive, 100-inch wheelbase, and weighed 600 pounds. Its price was $375. A unique feature was that the car could be started from the driver's seat by inserting a crank in the steering column.

The advertising copywriter's hyperbole reached a new height with the statement that, "Everyone has Speed protplasms in his blood and Motor Car driving is the universal systomic manifestation."

The Imp was built in 1913 and 1914 at the rate of about 50 per month in the plant at 500 Seventh Street in Auburn, which now houses Rieke Corporation. Several examples of the Imp are extant, including one at the Auburn Cord Duesenberg Museum.

IMPS, C. 1914. Harry McIntyre and Winthrop Ketchum stopped for a photograph with their Imps on the way to the 1914 Indianapolis 500.

AUBURN, C. 1910. Two gentlemen prepare to take their ladies for a ride in a new Auburn. Most cars were driven from the right side until 1912.

Ralph B. King, who was a bookkeeper for the W.H. Kiblinger Company and later the W.H. McIntyre Company, organized the King Motor Vehicle Company in 1908 to manufacture "a motor buggy especially designed for use of rural mail carriers." The Rural Free Delivery Act had just been passed by Congress and it seemed there might be a market for such a special vehicle. The enterprise did not last, however, and the company was out of business by 1909. No known example of the King has survived.

In 1908, Willis McDowell, Wheeler McDowell, and A.L. McDowell organized the McDowell Motor Vehicle Manufacturing Company with capital of $20,000. Their shop was in a brick building at the northeast corner of Main and Sixth Streets. A.L. McDowell had been an employee of the W.H. Kiblinger Company. Some sources doubt whether any cars were actually manufactured, but the company is listed as an automobile manufacturer in the 1908 Auburn Directory. No photographs or examples of this elusive Auburn-built vehicle are known.

In 1915, the Zimmerman Manufacturing Company was acquired by the Eckhart family. They organized the unincorporated Union Automobile Company and began building the Union automobile in the former Zimmerman plant on

North Indiana Avenue in Auburn under the supervision of John Zimmerman. All Auburn models were sixes, but the Union was a four—thus giving more range to the Auburn line. The enterprise was short-lived, the car continuing for only one season. No Union automobiles are extant.

The Auburn Automobile Company was clearly the strongest of the city's car companies. The company was well capitalized and was able to survive the vagaries of the economy and the automobile industry in general. Its automobiles were of solid design and construction. The company did not stray from its niche, as did McIntyre with the Imp during the cyclecar craze. Until 1906, Auburn cars were built in the Eckhart Carriage Company plant on East Seventh Street. One of these buildings has been preserved and moved to the National Automotive and Truck Museum of the United States at 1000 Gordon M. Buehrig Place.

In 1906, after the Model Gas Engine Works moved to Peru, Indiana, its complex of buildings was purchased by the Auburn Commercial Club and leased to the Auburn Automobile Company. These buildings were located at the south end of Main Street just south of the Vandalia Railroad. The main building is now used by the Auburn Street Department without its top story. The large walk-in vault still has the words "Auburn Automobile Company" in gilt on its door. Many large factory buildings were built subsequently at this location, some of which still stand as the Auburn Cord Duesenberg Museum and National Automotive and Truck Museum.

The 1903 cars were a bit more advanced and had pneumatic tires. A two-cylinder model was introduced in 1905 and a four-cylinder model in 1909. The five and six were offered in 1912. Auburn was a road-worthy car and competed well in the era when there were hundreds, if not thousands, of different makes available. The manufacturing, financial, and sales ability of Frank and Morris Eckhart added to the stability of the company.

Charles Eckhart began spending considerable time in the warm climate of California. Soon his sons followed and gradually became less interested in the company, although they had several excellent employees to run the day-to-day operations. Charles Eckhart and his sons were very generous to the city of Auburn. Their philanthropy included Eckhart Park, Eckhart Public Library, and the Young Men's Christian Association.

As automobiles became more sophisticated, manufacturers encouraged the building of good roads so that automobiles could be used for inter-city and long distance travel. They also encouraged the building of city parks so motorists had a place to stop for fresh water, toilet facilities, and to picnic or camp. The Eckharts practiced what they preached and created Eckhart Park for travelers into and through Auburn in 1915. The park was built for the use of persons traveling by automobile. It is indeed unfortunate that recent park boards have seen fit to scrap the ornate iron gates, to close the park to automobiles, and to destroy several of the drives through the park. It is hoped that city officials will eventually restore Eckhart Park to its original use as a park conducive and friendly to automobiles.

One of Auburn's more unusual industries was S.U. Tarney's "Positive Painless Pile Cure," which he sold by mail from his ornate brick residence at 603 South

Main Street. He also offered "Sovereign Balm" for Catarrh and Hay Fever and "Moss Rose" for "self treatment for the Ladies for diseases peculiar to their sex. Perfectly harmless." (And probably perfectly useless!)

In 1909, serious discussions were held toward building a library. Charles Eckhart offered to provide a site and an application was made to the Carnegie Corporation for a grant, which was later made in the amount of $15,500, based on the size of the population to be served. Eckhart did not feel that a library appropriate for the city of Auburn could be built for this sum and offered to build the library himself if the Carnegie agreement could be cancelled. The agreement was cancelled and steps were soon taken by Eckhart to proceed.

The library at Linton, Indiana had been chosen as a Carnegie model, but Eckhart wanted a unique building. Patton and Miller of Chicago were selected as architects to design the library. The design presented by them was Classic Chicago Prairie School architecture being pioneered at the time by the famous architect Frank Lloyd Wright.

The cornerstone was laid on May 13, 1910, with Governor Thomas Marshall presiding. J.A. McIntrye was master of ceremonies and the Auburn City Band played several numbers. Mayor Hugh Culbertson and Charles Eckhart both spoke. A reception in honor of Eckhart was given by W.H. McIntyre at his home at 703 South Main Street. Board members at that time were Charles Eckhart, J.A. McIntyre, E.A. Johnson, Willis Rhoads, Nellie Suckley, Mary Baxter, and Dr. Lida Leasure.

The building is a masterpiece of design and construction. It rests on a concrete foundation 4 feet wide, above which there is a 2-foot wall of concrete. The exterior is faced with Bedford limestone and salt-glazed brick. The roof is of green tile with broad overhangs. The entrances to the first floor are of marble and mosaic tile. The north stairway is of iron. The first floor trim is quarter-sawed oak. The second floor and basement are of red oak. Marble baseboards are used throughout. The buttresses on the four corners are counterpointed by the main entranceway. The windows are stained glass and of original design.

The site chosen was the east half of the block bounded by South Jackson, 12th, South VanBuren, and 13th Streets. The west half of this block had been the site of the old Auburn Academy and was then owned by the City of Auburn and used as a park. The west half of the block was later purchased from the city by Eckhart and donated to the library.

The cost of the building was in excess of $140,000. The library building was dedicated in January 1911 at the Methodist church. At the dedication, a letter was read from Professor Hippensteel, who had removed to Stevens Point, Wisconsin, where he brimmed with joy that the library which he had helped start finally had such a magnificent home.

Later, the Eckhart family purchased a cast iron fountain in Pittsburgh and had it erected on the west half of the block. An oil painting of Eckhart by R.W. Grafton of Richmond, Indiana was hung above the fireplace. The building and grounds were placed on the National Register of Historic Places in 1982.

COURTHOUSE OFFICIALS AND THOMAS MARSHALL. Future Indiana governor and United States Vice President Thomas Marshall (at the far right) was photographed at the west door of the 1865 courthouse.

The Eckhart Public Library has been actively used by its patrons over the years and is a monument to the foresight and generosity of Charles Eckhart. The building was extensively modified and an addition built in 1996.

The Young Men's Christian Association, now known simply as the YMCA or the "Y", originated as a result of the liquor business in Auburn in 1908. At that time, a number of prominent Auburn citizens mounted a campaign to rid the city of its nine saloons. Indiana had a local option law that enabled cities to become dry. An argument against the city's going dry was that the saloon was the working man's club and, if it was closed, the working man would have no place to go. To counteract this argument, it was felt that an alternative, such as a YMCA, should be established. With this reasoning, numerous discussions were held that resulted in Charles and Frank Eckhart offering $40,000 for the building of a YMCA if the community would guarantee an operating fund of $2,000 per year for five years. It was then estimated that operating expenses would be $6,000 per year, but that the remaining $4,000 would come from fees and other income.

This challenge was accepted and a board of directors was elected consisting of Charles Eckhart, Frank E. Eckhart, John Zimmerman, J.W. Sheffer, D.M. Hines, George Geugnot, R.A. Wilson, H.D. Weaver, J.I. Farley, B.O. Fink, and Larry Brandon.

Built on the site of the Pioneer Hotel Tavern, also known as the Auburn House, at the southeast corner of North Main and East Fifth Streets, the building was dedicated on April 12, 1914. It was designed by a firm of Chicago architects who specialized in YMCA buildings. The total cost of the building and equipment was $56,000 and was paid by the Eckharts as a gift to the city.

The original building had a number of sleeping rooms on the second and third floors, which were rented to young men who were working in Auburn. The YMCA also offered a gym, a pool, a bowling alley, a canteen, and a billiard parlor.

The Auburn institution was limited to men for the first several years of its operation. In 1918, the board of directors discussed opening the YMCA to women, but were discouraged by the national organization from taking this step. The board persisted, however, and on December 22, 1921, adopted a policy opening the facility to women and girls during certain days and months. The YMCA was a popular place for teenagers and the site of frequent dances, record hops, overnight swimming, basketball, volleyball, and similar activities.

On September 13, 1981, a larger new addition was dedicated containing a large gymnasium with a balcony track, a pool, two racquetball courts, a remodeled weight room, and new men's and women's locker rooms with saunas and whirlpools. A Nautilus Center was added in 1985. A second YMCA location containing a competitive pool, gymnasium, fitness center, locker rooms, and a daycare center was built in 1977 at 533 North Street.

The most magnificent building built during the era from 1900 to 1915 was the DeKalb County Courthouse. The 1864 brick courthouse had become inadequate

YMCA BUILDING. The Young Men's Christian Association was one of the first to admit women to activities.

for the fast-growing prosperous county. The many manufacturing companies and the yo-yo economy produced substantial property tax revenue. Many counties were building new courthouses. An elaborate courthouse was surely a source of community pride and a symbol of prosperity.

County officials decided to demolish the old courthouse and build a new one on the square. Demolition of the structure was a spectacular event. Strategically placed charges of dynamite quickly removed the octagonal tower that had been a DeKalb County landmark for almost half a century.

DeKalb County citizens and officials had talked about a new courthouse for many years. While the brick courthouse with its octagonal tower was a handsome building, it had become too small for the county's needs and some feared that it was not a safe place for the deposit of county records.

A new county infirmary was needed also. After considerable discussions, it was concluded that the infirmary should be built first because it could be paid for over a relatively short period of time. Thereafter, the new courthouse could be built. The County Infirmary (now called DeKalb County Farm) was completed in 1908.

DeKalb County continued to grow. The first decade of the century was particularly prosperous and progressive. Electric lights and telephones became available in Auburn. Interurban lines made distant communities conveniently close. The automobile was developing as a means of transportation. There were multiple automobile manufacturers in Auburn and all were doing well. A new courthouse was a symbol of community progress and a matter of great pride. The desire for a new courthouse intensified and it soon became apparent that it would be financially possible.

The first organized effort toward building a new courthouse began on Friday, August 13, 1909, when the Auburn Commercial Club (predecessor to the Auburn Chamber of Commerce) called a meeting of its directors "to discuss ways and means and plans whereby DeKalb County might have a courthouse suitable of the needs of the county, a place where records would be safe from the ravages of fire and in keeping with the wealth of the county."

This group decided to request the DeKalb County Commissioners to make requisition for funds to prepare plans and specifications for the new building in time for the DeKalb County Council to act on it at their September meeting. They had to act quickly in order to get this accomplished, so they formed an "automobile party" that afternoon and drove to the home of their commissioner, Thomas F. Elson, to discuss the matter. Elson agreed to call a special meeting of the commissioners. The commissioners met on August 16, 1909 and made an appropriation of $1,000, of which $200 was to be available in 1909 for the inspection of other buildings and $800 was to be used for preparing plans and specifications. The DeKalb County Council met on September 9, 1909 and appropriated $200 to provide for the inspection of other buildings. The County Infirmary had been paid for with a tax levy of 44¢ per $100 valuation. The council decided to leave this levy in effect in order to accumulate funds for the new courthouse.

As county officials began serious planning for a new courthouse, Waterloo citizens renewed their prior efforts to move the county seat to their town. On February 25, 1910, the *Waterloo Press* reported that 50 to 60 people attended a meeting of the Waterloo Commercial Club the prior Tuesday whereby efforts were initiated for this purpose. Two committees were appointed, one to look into the legalities and the other to raise funds for the effort. H.D. Boozer and W.H. Leas each subscribed $1,000. The editor opined that he would not object "if they keep within the $250,000 figure on which the project was first put up to the people." He observed, however, that "Auburn people are enthusiastic for the new courthouse, of course, and they will be different from the common run of mortals if they don't secure just as costly a building as possible."

The commissioners began inspecting courthouses in other counties and were soon ready to express their preferences to architects. They met with several prospective architects on February 13, 1910. The firm of Mahurin and Mahurin of Fort Wayne was selected on February 15, 1910 and instructed to begin preparing plans in accordance with the preferences of the commissioners.

The prominent firm was a wise choice for the design of the DeKalb County Courthouse. Members of the firm were Marshall S. Mahurin and his nephew Guy M. Mahurin. The former had been orphaned at an early age and thereafter resided in Auburn with a sister. Mahurin started with the architectural firm of T.J. Tolan and Son, designers of the Allen County Courthouse. After Tolan's death, Mahurin began working with a Tolan employee, John F. Wing, and later formed a partnership, Wing and Mahurin, which continued until 1907 when the Mahurin and Mahurin firm was formed.

This firm specialized in public buildings such as courthouses, jails, schools, and churches. The Mahurins designed the courthouses at Michigan City and Bloomington, Indiana, the Fort Wayne Scottish Rite Cathedral, a Ball residence at Muncie, and many other prominent buildings.

The estimated cost was to be $250,000. Requisition in this amount was made by the commissioners in August 1910, and an appropriation in a like amount was made by the council at their September meeting. A bond issue of $150,000 to be paid over a period of ten years at 3.5 percent interest was also approved. The county had a surplus of $100,000 to be applied to the construction cost and was otherwise debt free.

Contractors were invited to bid on the project, and ten bids were received. They were opened May 4, 1911 and the bid of J.B. Goodall of Peru, Indiana, in the amount of $185,000 for the basic construction, was accepted.

After the demolition of the brick courthouse and before the completion of the present limestone courthouse, a temporary courthouse was established in a building between West Eighth and West Ninth streets along the east side of South Jackson Street. At that time, the W.H. McIntyre Company Automobile Plants One and Two were located along the east side of South Jackson Street. Although extensively modified, the north building still stands and is the location of the present Auburn House Restaurant at 131 West Seventh Street. The south building was identical and was connected to the north building by bridges extending over West Eighth Street at both the second- and third-story levels.

The south portion of the south building was used as a temporary courthouse. All court offices and records had been moved to the building. It was ideal for the purpose because of its size, central location, and the fact that it had a large walk-in vault for record storage. A crude courtroom was established in a large storage room.

On the evening of February 8, 1913, the south building burned in the most disastrous fire DeKalb County has ever known. The alarm was sounded about dusk and the whole town turned out to help fight the fire. The water supply was soon exhausted. So little could be done as the flames spread throughout the three-story building. Firefighters and citizens concentrated on retrieving as much as possible from the burning building. Fortunately, most county records were saved. Most important were the recorder's records, which affected the titles to real estate. The only records lost completely were those of the office of clerk of the circuit court.

Records that were saved were quickly moved to the partially completed courthouse and temporary offices were established there. Necessity pressed the new building into service before it was completed.

DEMOLITION OF COURTHOUSE TOWER. *The octagonal tower that welcomed Civil War soldiers back to Auburn was imploded with dynamite.*

LAYING THE CORNERSTONE OF THE DEKALB COUNTY COURTHOUSE. The cornerstone was laid on July 27, 1911 with appropriate ceremonies.

The burned building also housed many other businesses. The McIntyre Automobile Salesroom lost five McIntyre cars, the Double Fabric Tire Company lost most of its assets, and the *Auburn Courier* lost all but some typewriters and office equipment.

Demolition of the old courthouse began on May 8, 1911. The work progressed rapidly, with as many as 50 men being employed on the project at one time.

Cornerstone laying ceremonies were held on Thursday, July 27, 1911. The program began at 10:30 a.m. and lasted through the afternoon. The program commenced with music by the Waterloo, Garrett, and Auburn bands. The cornerstone weighed 5 tons and was laid by the DeKalb Lodge No. 214, Free and Accepted Masons. William Geake, Deputy Grand Marshall of Indiana, was the master of ceremonies and addressed the crowd first.

After a dinner break, those gathered were addressed by J.D. Leighty, Judge Frank M. Powers, Newton W. Gilbert, and Governor Thomas R. Marshall. J.D. Leighty was chairman of the Arrangements Committee and gave a historical sketch of the old courthouse. Frank M. Powers was the Circuit Court judge for DeKalb and Steuben Counties and spoke generally on justice and liberty. Newton W. Gilbert was vice-governor of the Philippines.

The principal speaker of the day was Governor Thomas R. Marshall of Columbia City. He was well acquainted in Auburn and had appeared in DeKalb Circuit Court many times. The governor was introduced by J.D. Leighty:

> We have with us today, an honored citizen of a nearby county. One who has often practiced his profession in the court of this county; one who by ability and forceful eloquence has attained high standing throughout the county; one who has been chosen by the people of our state to the highest place within their gift; one who is a prospective candidate for his party for the place of greatest honor, trust, and power that can be conferred on any man—the Presidency of the United States.

Governor Marshall had been popular throughout the state and had gained considerable national recognition. He had announced his candidacy for President just a week before. His address was the first since he had made the announcement and was clearly that of a national candidate. The content of the speech is striking, in that the speech could be given by a present-day presidential or vice presidential candidate and be almost wholly applicable to present issues—law and order, individual freedom, energy, government control, the power of the courts, and consumer protection.

Marshall campaigned on these themes throughout the country. His chief opponent was Woodrow Wilson of New Jersey. After 26 ballots at the 1912 Democratic Convention, Wilson and Marshall were deadlocked, neither with enough votes to prevail. Marshall then agreed to give his votes to Wilson in exchange for the vice presidential nomination. The ticket was elected. Marshall had a distinguished political career, but ironically is remembered most for this statement: "What this country needs is a really good five-cent cigar."

Work progressed steadily on the huge courthouse building. It was even more beautiful than the architect's renderings. The courthouse is modern Ionic Greek architecture. The shape of the building is a parallelogram with a frontage of 140 feet on the east and west, and a depth of 116 feet on the north and south. It covers 18,000 square feet and its three floors total 54,000 square feet, or about 1.25 acres. The total height is 56 feet and it contains 1,170,000 cubic feet.

The first floor is 14 feet high and is five steps above ground level. The first floor level originally contained the sheriff's office, surveyor's office, assessor's office, custodian's room, stale record room, an assembly hall that seated 600 people, a "Women's Rest and Retiring Room," and a "Men's Public Toilet Room."

The second floor is also 14 feet high and contains the auditor's, treasurer's, recorder's, and clerk's offices, and the Commissioners' Court.

The third floor is 13 feet high and originally contained two courtrooms, a law library, GAR room, county school, superintendent's rooms, grand jury room, petit jury room, and witness room.

The circuit courtroom is 40 feet by 60 feet and has a ceiling height of 25 feet. Originally, the entire ceiling was of Florentine glass under a skylight. Because the acoustics were considered poor, the Florentine glass was covered with acoustical tile in 1961.

The building is faced with Indiana Oolitic Limestone over brick. The interior columns, floors, and roof are reinforced concrete and all interior partitions are made of gypsum blocks. The corridor floors are encaustic tile and the offices are marblithic tile. The courtroom and original law library floors were cork tile. The corridor wainscoting and the stairs are built of Vermont marble.

The interior columns are scaliola, and the walls and ceilings are beautifully decorated to resemble marble. This process was carried out by a crew of Italian decorators brought in from the east.

The only wood in the building is in the commissioners' and circuit courtrooms' wall paneling. All of the doors, casings, trim, and all counters, furniture, files, and shelving are made of steel grained to imitate oak wood.

The large brass master clock located on the first floor controlled the exterior pediment clocks and 22 secondary clocks located throughout the building by means of air tubes. An impulse of air is sent forth every alternate minute and inflates the diaphragm of the secondary clocks. The opening of the valves in the master clock in alternate minutes releases the impulse and allows all air in the tubing system to equalize. Thus, all secondary clocks are moved forward a minute at a time. The time-keeping system was manufactured by the Hahl Automatic Clock Company of Chicago. The pediment clocks were electrified in recent years.

Both gas and electric lights were installed when the building was built. Natural gas was plentiful in Auburn at the time, but electricity prevailed. The gas fixtures may still be seen. A central vacuum cleaning system is no longer used. The roof was originally red tile, but has been replaced by copper. A flagpole capped by an American Eagle was originally installed on top of the building.

The Florentine glass dome is a sight to behold. It is wholly contained within the attic level and is illuminated by skylights during the day and electric lights at night.

The building contains 473 carloads of material and weighs approximately 11,301 tons. The total cost, including furnishings, was $317,072.14.

The mural paintings on each side of the landing between the second and third stories are a principal feature of the DeKalb County Courthouse. They are 18 feet in width and 12 feet in height. The murals were painted in New York City by Arthur Thomas, who was born in Dresden, Germany in 1858 and came to the United States in 1893. Thomas also did the murals on either side of the bench in the circuit courtroom. They are allegorical of justice and liberty.

The DeKalb County Courthouse was designed and built to serve this county for many years. It has provided sufficient room for growth while most other counties have found themselves cramped for office space. The foresight of those who designed and built the courthouse is attested to by the fact that a second courtroom was provided. It was not utilized until 1976, when the DeKalb County Court was established.

The DeKalb County Commissioners have very carefully maintained the building and it continues to be a beautiful courthouse that will serve DeKalb County for many more years.

After almost five years of planning and building, the DeKalb County Courthouse was completed. A dedication ceremony befitting the occasion was arranged and held on Thursday, June 18, 1914. The *Evening Star* reported:

COURTHOUSE ROTUNDA. The courthouse rotunda area with its backlit art-glass dome and faux marble is a beautiful sight.

Amid the cheering of thousands of people, the playing of bands and the fluttering of flags, DeKalb County's new $300,000 courthouse was dedicated with appropriate exercise this afternoon.

From early in the morning until late in the afternoon, streams of people poured into the county seat to witness the ceremonies in connection with the dedication of the second finest courthouse in the State of Indiana. The crowd late this afternoon was estimated at 10,000 to 15,000 people.

The dedication proper opened with a band concert by the Auburn City Band from 8:45 to 9:10. At 9:10 the band formed a line and marched to the Vandalia Depot to meet the Butler delegation. At 9:45 the Auburn Band marched to the Lakeshore Depot to meet the Angola delegation, while the Butler band played a concert at the bandstand.

The Old Settlers had their program in the morning, and an unusually large number were present. The Hon. Newton Gilbert, of Angola, recently the Vice-Governor of the Philippines, made the chief address of

> the day. The biographers report showed that an unusually large number of Old Settlers died during the past year.
>
> During the noon hour the bands played concerts, the Butler Band from 12:00 to 12:30, the Auburn Band from 12:30 to 1:00, and the Garrett Band from 1:00 to 1:30. At 1:30 all the bands formed a line in front of the Swineford Hotel and escorted the speakers to the stand.
>
> The Royal Black Hussar Band of Auburn opened the afternoon program with a short concert, which was followed by a song by a chorus. After the invocation of Rev. J.G. Wise and a duet by H.C. McClung and F.A. Pribbenow, Judge Frank M. Powers addressed the audience. The Quinque Quartette of Waterloo followed with a song, after which the building was formally dedicated by the noted jurist, Judge John W. Hannan of LaGrange. The program was concluded by the raising of the American flag, a song by the chorus, and a fire drill by the Auburn Fire Department.

The general contractor J.B. Goodall delivered the key to the building to the architect Marshall S. Mahurin, who in turn presented it to the DeKalb County Commissioners. The board presented the key to Judge Frank M. Powers, who presented it to the Honorable John W. Hannan, orator of the day, with the request that he dedicate the DeKalb County Courthouse to "Utility, Justice, and Liberty."

AUTOMOBILES AND INTERURBAN TRACKS. East Seventh Street is in the foreground, and the interurban tracks run down the middle of Cedar Street. The 1865 courthouse is on the right. McIntyre cars are on the left, Auburn cars are in the middle, and Zimmerman cars are on the right.

The Royal Black Hussars was an Auburn band that played on the Lincoln Chautauqua System throughout the Midwest. The *Evening Star* reported, "The seventeen musicians played as one man and to sum up their work in two words, one has but to say that this is 'Some Band.' Their work was highly appreciated, not only by officials in charge of the day's program but the throngs that stood spellbound throughout their concert."

Thousands came to Auburn for the occasion. The *Evening Star* noted, "Automobiles lined Main Street from north to south, and the side streets were filled with machines. Never before were there so many automobiles seen in Auburn at one time."

The Shannon Stock Company was in town with a tent show, "The Village Gossips," and Auburn merchants enjoyed the influx of people. Beidler's Shoe Store advertised the following:

> We have had made especially for Dedication Day a beautiful oval pocket mirror with a picture in colors on back of DeKalb County's New Courthouse. To every Man or Woman who will come in our store and register, we will give one of these beautiful souvenirs. They will be useful and be a constant reminder of DeKalb County's Best and Largest Shoe Store where We Fit Your Feet.

The dedication program was full of the customary pomp and ceremony of the day, but the DeKalb County Courthouse has clearly lived up to the purpose for which it was dedicated: "Utility, Justice, and Liberty."

The last railroad built in DeKalb County was the interurban system. Indiana led the nation in the amount of interurban trackage. It was a fantastic transportation system, which was generally very prompt and efficient.

The word interurban was coined in 1893 by Charles L. Henry, a lawyer from Anderson, Indiana, who was an electric rail pioneer. The concept of individual electrically-powered cars that could operate quickly and efficiently to move passengers and freight from one town to another soon caught on.

Fort Wayne became a hub for the emerging interurban companies. The first service out of Fort Wayne began on December 12, 1901 when a car went from Fort Wayne to Huntington. Many companies were established to provide service in and out of Fort Wayne.

One of the most ambitious companies was the Toledo and Chicago Interurban Railway Company, which was incorporated on March 26, 1903 with capital of $500,000, later raised to $1.25 million on April 26, 1905. The company planned to build an interurban railroad from Toledo to Chicago. Their first step was to build the Fort Wayne Division. This line would connect their proposed main line, which would presumably have paralleled the New York Central right-of-way, to the other companies' lines, which converged at Fort Wayne.

The main line from Toledo to Chicago never materialized, but the Fort Wayne Division was to become very important to the growth and development of DeKalb

County. The trackage came north from Fort Wayne along the east and then the west side of the Lima Road, now State Road 3, to Huntertown; then northeast cross country to a gravel operation at what is now called the Indian Springs area; then along the west side of what is now State Road 327 for a stretch; and finally into Garrett.

At Cowen and King Streets, the tracks split at Transfer Corner. One line went northwest to Avilla and then north to Kendallville, and the other line went east to Auburn and then north to Waterloo.

The line to Auburn was on the south right of way of County Road 48 and then down the middle of Ensley Avenue to Cedar Street. Its route went down the middle of Cedar Street to State Road 427 and then along the east right of way of State Road 427 to a point near DeKalb High School, where it crossed County Road 427 and continued along the west side into Waterloo.

The interurban station at Auburn was first located in the building at the northwest corner of East Seventh and Cedar Streets. Later, a modern station and terminal building were built on the northeast corner of Cedar and 12th Streets. Connections were made at Waterloo with the Lakeshore & Michigan Southern and Fort Wayne, Jackson & Saginaw ; at Auburn with the Eel River, then Vandalia; at Auburn Junction with the Baltimore & Ohio, the Fort Wayne, Jackson & Saginaw, and again with the Eel River, then Vandalia lines; at Garrett with the Baltimore & Ohio; and at Cedar again with the Eel River, then the Vandalia. There were also a number of stations where passengers could board or leave the cars. For that matter, the car would usually stop anywhere on request.

The railroads generally opposed the attempts of the Toledo and Chicago to connect with their lines. For example, at Waterloo the competing railroads built fences along their lines so interurban passengers had a difficult time getting to the connecting lines.

The first cars to provide service were run through DeKalb County on May 10, 1906. Hourly service was widely accepted, but the usage did not meet company expectations due mainly to the resistance of the established railroads at connecting points.

As a result, the Toledo and Chicago Interurban Railway went into receivership in 1908 and was eventually sold at foreclosure sale on April 12, 1913, for $550,000 to the Fort Wayne and Northwestern Railway Company, a corporation named by the company's bondholders. The sale included 18.9 miles of track in DeKalb County and seven passenger units, six power and one trailing; nine freight units, two power and seven trailing; and ten service units, four power and one trailing.

The Fort Wayne and Northwestern Railway Company had been incorporated on April 12, 1913, specifically to purchase the defunct Toledo and Chicago. Its capitalization was $1.95 million. This company enjoyed modest success. In 1916, it provided 109,241 freight car miles.

On October 1, 1924, the line was sold to the Indiana Service Corporation, the successor to the Fort Wayne and Northern Indiana Traction Company. This company incorporated on January 15, 1920, with a capital of $10 million, and

INTERURBAN AND AUBURN TEST CAR. These vehicles are headed east on County Road 48. The Baltimore & Ohio Railroad tracks are in the foreground. Note the wires that provided electricity to the interurban.

proceeded to purchase a number of the lines converging in Fort Wayne. At its peak in 1929, it carried 26,175,378 passengers.

On August 1, 1930, operation of the rail lines was transferred to the Indiana Railroad System, which had been incorporated on July 2, 1930 for the purpose of operating most of the interurban lines in Indiana on a consolidated basis. At the peak of its short but active life, it was the largest interurban system in the world.

The Depression, along with the more widespread use of the automobile for short distance trips and trucks for short distance hauling, resulted in the decline of the demand for interurban travel and shipping. Passenger service in DeKalb County was discontinued on February 15, 1937 and freight service to Garrett on May 10, 1945. Freight service was retained to haul coal for the Indiana and Michigan Electric Company generating plant in Fort Wayne from the Vandalia and Baltimore & Ohio trackage. This was the last interurban service out of Fort Wayne.

Interurban travel was quick, easy, and inexpensive. A passenger could board a car at Waterloo at 7:50 a.m., be in Fort Wayne at 8:21 a.m., leave Fort Wayne at 4:39 p.m., and arrive back at Waterloo at 6:05 p.m. Connections could easily be made to go to Indianapolis, Louisville, or any city in between.

Light freight was also hauled. Wholesale grocers in Fort Wayne sent their wares to DeKalb County Merchants by interurban. A phone call to Fort Wayne could result in goods being received within two hours, certainly faster service than today.

The interurban was also used to ship farm produce. For example, farmers along the line raised cabbage for the sauerkraut factory at Auburn Junction and shipped the crates of cabbage by interurban. Milk, cream, and eggs were also shipped regularly.

CAR LINE. This interurban car is shown on the square along South Cedar Street. The 1865 courthouse is in the left background and the north side of the square is in the right background.

The interurban cars were operated by electricity, which was generated by the companies themselves. The Toledo and Chicago Interurban Railway Company envisioned a large system from Toledo to Chicago with connections at Kendallville and Waterloo through Garrett to Fort Wayne. As part of this grand scheme, they built a large coal-fired steam electric generating plant on the shores of Bixler Lake at Kendallville. This plant was to power a large part of the system. There were also several stations, including one in the building at Cedar and 12th Streets in Auburn.

Initially, the system was powered by a 3,300-volt alternating current system. This was indeed a very powerful system and would have been profitable had the lines actually been built from Toledo to Chicago. When the system was sold to the Fort Wayne and Northwestern Railway Company in 1913, the system was changed to a 600-volt direct current system, which had become the standard interurban voltage. This necessitated putting new motors and controls in the cars, making them much lighter and easier to operate with fast accelerations and quick stops. An approaching car could be detected by the humming of the overhead wires and by the blue arc of the car connectors sliding along the overhead wires.

With the decline of the interurban system, the companies began selling their excess power and soon got into the electric business. The Indiana Service Company was acquired by the Indiana and Michigan Electric Company and became the nucleus of their electric system in DeKalb and Noble Counties.

The infrastructure of the streets, sewers, waterlines, and electrical service was well in place by 1915. John Zimmerman, one of the councilmen elected after Auburn became a city, did extensive research among many vendors and other cities to determine what was best for Auburn. Streets and curbs were built. Electric service was available throughout the city.

Domestic life had become much easier. Most homes had electric lights and municipal water and sewer service. Many homes had telephones. Automobiles were in general use although the Interurban and railroads were still the transportation modes of choice for long distance travel.

While we revere the quality of the cars built in Auburn, one should not forget that they were built by hundreds of dedicated workmen and a few women. The First Annual Report of the 1912 Indiana State Bureau of Inspection reported that Auburn Automobile Company employed 160 men and 3 women; W.H. McIntyre Company employed 72 men and 5 women; and Zimmerman Manufacturing Company employed 72 men and 8 women. All worked 60 hours per week. The work was hard, the hours long, and the conditions less then desirable considering the lack of air conditioning in summer and only nominal heat in winter.

Nevertheless, it was employment. The jobs provided an income to support a family and to "get ahead." Auburn's automobile industry attracted workers to Auburn. The author's grandfather, Walter Creager, commuted weekly from Whitley County to work at the W.H. McIntyre Company. He rented a room with board through the week.

While the automobile industry was dominant, other industry, collateral and unrelated, continued to develop. The Auburn Foundry was established in 1911 and was located at 635 West 11th Street. The Auburn Foundry made gray iron castings used by the local automobile industry.

The Double Fabric Tire Company was organized in 1913 and made "Interlocks" for automobile tires. These were inserted into tires between the inner tire and the tube to protect the tire from the bad roads of the time. In about 1919 the company started making tires under the "Auburn" name.

The Auburn Concrete Machinery Company was formed in 1904 and the Concrete Block Manufacturing Company was founded in 1906. The new technology of concrete enabled the casting of cement blocks in various decorative forms. There are many houses built in Auburn of these blocks. The building at the northwest corner of North Eighth and South Main Streets is faced with a thin block with a decorative surface. These provided a "modern" look to an old brick building.

Three additional wood product companies were formed—the Auburn Excelsior Company (1901) made excelsior (fine wood shavings), used for packing in crates; the Auburn Hardwood Company (1902) sawed logs into dimension lumber, much of which was used in the manufacturing of buggies and automobiles; and the Auburn Handle Factory (1906) manufactured various handles for axes, picks, etc.

Three cigar companies were formed in 1908 to hand-make cigars from raw tobacco shipped from Cuba and southern states. These were Hull and Hull Cigar

Company, Brugh and Shaw Cigar Company, and John Koons Cigar Company, whose brands included "Bankers' Daughter, Victor Joe, and Receipt."

Berg's Bottling Works was established in 1908 to manufacture and bottle soda pop. Also in 1908, the Auburn Carpet Company made carpet from cloth scraps.

On September 15, 1910, the Whitten-Dennison Post Card Company moved to Auburn. They built a small factory on East Seventh Street adjacent to Cedar Creek, which employed five "girls." A major fire destroyed the company in 1913, but a structure was soon built to replace it. By 1913, the name of the company was changed to Auburn Post Card Manufacturing Company. The initial product of the company was postcards, which were immensely popular from about 1900 into the 1920s, as postal regulations were changed to permit cards with messages.

Despite the prominence of the automobile industry, carriage production continued in Auburn. Zimmerman Manufacturing Company continued to build buggies until 1909 when it sold its line of "Blue Ribbon" vehicles to the Eckhart Carriage Company. Eckhart continued to build between 4,000 and 5,000 units a year until a disastrous fire destroyed much of the factory on East Seventh Street in January 1913. Despite the fire, production continued until 1918. In 1915, the company manufactured a "jitney bus" body, which would fit onto a Ford Chassis. An advertisement in the November 1915 issue of *Motor Bus* magazine stated that the bodies were "Equipped with rain vision ventilating windshield, electric domelight, gasoline tank . . . good clear American window glass . . . adjustable for winter or summer use, side entrance, rear exit." The bus would seat seven passengers regularly, nine if necessary. The W.H. Kiblinger/McIntyre Company continued to build carriages until about 1912.

THE FLYING SQUADRON—JUNE 11, 1912. Auburn automobile manufacturers parked their current models on the west side of the square for "Auburn Bargain Week."

6. Reality, Hope, and Honest Endeavor: Recession and War (1916–1925)

Auburn Forever with Honest Endeavor.

~Motto of Auburn Commercial Club

The bubble had burst. Intense competition, strategic errors, and economic recession led to the gradual attrition of the automobile industry. Only Auburn Automobile Company remained relatively strong. The others had failed or were failing.

War along the Mexican border and in Europe preoccupied our citizens. The dependence on coal as a fuel made a miner's strike disastrous. The death of two of Auburn's leading citizens, Charles Eckhart and W.H. McIntyre, left a void of leadership, vision, and, in the case of Charles Eckhart, philanthropy.

A new Auburn City Hall and DeKalb County Jail were built side by side on Cedar Street east of the square. A new high school building was built at the 700 block of South Main Street.

After the death of their father, the Eckhart brothers, Frank and Morris, lost interest in the Auburn Automobile Company, preferring the climate of California, to which they had traveled many times to demonstrate the efficiency of the automobile for cross-country travel. They left the company in the hands of trusted employees, but when the opportunity came, sold it to a group of Chicago investors. While the company faltered under absentee ownership, the Chicago group had the good sense and fortune to put it in the hands of the unknown and brash but visionary E.L. Cord. Auburn would rise again!

During this era, the federal government made two major changes in the lives of our citizens, one successful and the other a failure—women's suffrage and prohibition.

In 1916, Mexican revolutionary Pancho Villa led a guerilla band in raids into New Mexico and Texas, killing 17 Americans. The United States Army under the command of General John J. Pershing led troops into the border conflict. Local Indiana National Guard troops under the command of Colonel Aubrey Kuhlman were sent to assist.

The culmination of festering relations between Eastern European countries and the assassination of Archduke Francis Ferdinand, heir to the throne of Austria-Hungary, at Sarajevo on June 28, 1914, led to the start of World War I.

Austria-Hungary blamed the assassination plot on its neighbor Serbia and declared war against Serbia on July 28, 1914. By October 30, 1914, the Central Powers—Austria-Hungary, Germany, and the Ottoman Empire—were at war with the Allies: Belgium, France, Great Britain, Russia, and Serbia.

News of the outbreak of war surprised most Americans. President Woodrow Wilson declared that the United States would be "neutral in fact as well as name." In 1915, a German submarine torpedoed the *Lusitania*, killing 126 Americans. Wilson was determined to remain neutral, but began making preparations for war just in case.

In January 1917, the British intercepted a message from Germany to Mexico indicating that Germany had offered Mexico an alliance in case of war with the United States and, in exchange, promised to help Mexico recover land it had ceded to the United States after the Mexican War. This alerted the United States to the plans of Germany. Frequent sinking of United States merchant ships resulted in a declaration of war against Germany on April 6, 1917.

Reacting very quickly to the declaration of war, Auburn citizens held a patriotic rally on the courthouse square on April 9, 1917, with Mayor J.Y.W. McClellan presiding and patriotic speeches given by Judge Dan M. Link and Captain A.L. Moody of Company K.

Various committees were formed to assist in recruiting. A recruiting tent was established on the courthouse lawn on April 12, 1917, where it remained until May 9, 1917. Soon, 47 men attempted to enlist, with 12 rejected due to physical problems and 35 accepted for service. Miss Nellie Harding volunteered for the ambulance corps of the Red Cross.

Company K, still functioning and the focus of the recruiting activity, was formally mustered in on August 9, 1917. On August 10, 1917, Company K left Auburn for Fort Benjamin Harrison from the New York Central Depot located on the north side of West Seventh Street. The company marched to the station from the square led by bands and fife and drum corps. Patriotic speeches were made. The crowd numbered in excess of 4,000 people.

In September 1917, Company K was sent to Camp Shelby at Hattiesburg, Mississippi, and was later transferred to the Depot Brigade, becoming Company 10 of the brigade. Later, the company lost its identity and became part of the 151st Indiana Infantry, with the officers and men transferred therein. The officers of Company K when they left Auburn were Captain Walter D. Stump, First Lieutenant Walter A. Lobmiller, Second Lieutenant Glen W. Wetzel, First Sergeant Samuel McIntosh, Superior Sergeant Henry Imhoff, and Mess Sergeant Kenneth Walter.

The draft law was passed by Congress on April 28, 1917 and Governor James P. Goodrich appointed Sheriff Frank Baltz, County Clerk W.W. Mountz, and I.M. Zent as members of the conscription board. The next step was to register all eligible DeKalb County men. This was accomplished by a registrar in each political precinct. The Registrars reported 2,054 were registered with 1,457 exemptions filed, leaving 597 eligible.

The first draft was held July 20, 1917 and the first name drawn was Lee W. Hodges of Waterloo. The quota for DeKalb County was 218 men, the number already in Company K, which was approximately 100 men, and the number who had volunteered to that point, leaving about 80 to be drafted. Those who were drafted had the option of volunteering with Company K, which Captain Stump encouraged so that he could bring the number up to the full 150 men before muster.

On July 25, 1917, it was announced that DeKalb County must supply 88 men for the new National Army, after getting credit for 41 enlistments in the regular army and 119 enlistments in the Indiana National Guard. Later, the number was increased to 97.

Many DeKalb County men were decorated. Among them were Lieutenant George Carroll of Garrett who was awarded the highest French decoration for bravery—the Croix de Guerre, with the Palm and Star.

Twenty-three DeKalb County soldiers gave the supreme sacrifice for the good of their country. Their photographs hang in the east stairwell of the courthouse.

WORLD WAR I SOLDIERS. Recruits in uniform pose for a photograph. World War I infantrymen were known as "Doughboys."

The people of Auburn supported the war effort from the beginning in every conceivable way. The Citizen's Defense League was organized to promote recruiting and other patriotic purposes. The officers were Major J.Y.W. McClellan, chairman; W.D. Stump, secretary; and I.M. Zent, treasurer.

The DeKalb County Red Cross Chapter was organized and a charter sought from the National Red Cross. Judge Dan M. Link was selected chairman and 36 directors were named, each township, town, and city being represented. The organization raised $7,600 within two months for the war fund of the American Red Cross. Over 2,000 DeKalb County people became members. The women of the organization obtained the use of the Assembly Room in the courthouse and began making hospital supplies. In 1918, another fund drive raised $18,588 against a quota of $15,000.

The production and conservation of food was a primary concern. The Citizen's Defense League planted the vacant lots in Auburn and encouraged residents to plant war gardens on their land. Five car loads of seed potatoes were obtained and sold at cost. Sugar was rationed. W.A. Thomas of the Thomas Baking Company of Auburn standardized the bread loaf and was able to decrease the cost by 2¢ per pound. The DeKalb County Food Administration later formalized some of these activities.

The Auburn YMCA raised $15,000 for Army and Navy work. Several DeKalb County men assisted the YMCA in their work with the troops.

Funds for the war effort were borrowed from the nation's patriotic citizens in the form of Liberty Loans. I.M. Zent was chairman of the committee and the

SOLDIERS' MONUMENT AND JAIL. An iron fence surrounded the monument. Note the cannonballs welded into a pyramid. The livery stable is to the left of the jail.

presidents of the several banks in the county were members. By June 13, 1917, bonds in the amount of $279,200 had been sold against a goal of $252,000. The second quota was requested in October in the amount of $340,000. The last quota was set at $650,000 and $818,600 was raised. After the war was over, the government still had huge deficits, so the Victory Loan Campaign, to which DeKalb County subscribed $512,800, was established. The Liberty Loan drives were successful largely because of the efforts of V.E. Buchanan, general manager of the Auburn Printing Company. Many novel means were used to publicize the campaign, including flights over DeKalb County by the famous aviator, Art Smith. The Women's Liberty Loan Committee was also of great assistance.

War Savings Stamps were another means of borrowing money from the people. These stamps, in denominations as low as 10¢, brought sales of $552,000 during the war. Many patriotic citizens spoke at meetings throughout the events in support of the drive.

The DeKalb County Fuel Administrator was W.H. Mountz of Garrett. Local distributors were appointed for coal. The use of gasoline and kerosene was curtailed. Farmers were encouraged to cut wood and sell it to reduce the use of coal.

The Boys' Working Reserve was organized to place boys under military age in posts that had been vacated by older men. W.A. Benford was director of the program. The DeKalb County United War Workers and the Victory Girls were organized to promote the war effort among civilian workers.

The DeKalb County Home Guard Company was organized in July 1917 to stimulate patriotism and to emphasize the realization of a state of war. Captain L.L. Denison of Garrett was appointed chairman. The company met once per week and drilled for about two months, but was soon disbanded from lack of interest.

One of the most difficult civilian positions was that of United States Appeal Agent, which was held by Herbert C. Willis of Waterloo. It was his responsibility to hear the appeals of those who were drafted. A Committee on Disloyalty was established in August 1917. This later evolved into a chapter of the American Protective League, a secret organization.

The Citizen's Defense League continued to help conserve money and material. All enterprises were tested by the criteria "Will this help with the war?" Later, permits were required before construction of any kind could be undertaken.

The entry of the United States into the war tipped the scales in favor of the Allies and resulted in the signing of an armistice on November 11, 1918. The war was of relatively short duration, but the citizens of DeKalb County were still very relieved when it was over. Celebrations were held in all of our towns.

On October 9, 1919, the American Legion of DeKalb County was organized with 30 charter members and a national charter requested.

After the courthouse was built in 1913, the old 1873 jail still stood on the southeast corner of the square. There was also a public toilet adjacent to the jail facing Cedar Street. The old jail was an eyesore on the square and was in need of substantial repairs. Therefore, the county commissioners voted to build a new jail. The contract was let on May 28, 1917 to H.H. Ackemere of Auburn for $52,940. The final cost was $89,535. The new jail was first occupied on January 15, 1918 and was in service until 1985.

The new jail was located at the southeast corner of Cedar and Eighth Streets. It was contemporary to the Commercial Building on its north and to the Auburn City Hall on its south and was built of the latest and most advanced design. The sheriff's residence was in the front facing the square. It was a functional but pleasing residence. Second-floor bedrooms were located on the northwest and southwest corners. Each bedroom was adorned with an original oil painting of a landscape scene above a fireplace.

As originally built, the jail portion contained sixteen cells, there being eight on each floor in two rows of four each. There was also a juvenile ward of two rooms on the first floor. On the second floor, there was a women's ward, a hospital, and insane ward.

The city hall at the northeast corner of South Cedar and East Ninth Streets was actually the former DeKalb County Jail building that had been moved from the square when the 1873 jail was built. It was a large frame building that housed city government and the Auburn Fire Department, including its two teams of five horses and a supply of hay and grain.

During the administration of Mayor Hugh Culbertson, a new city hall was built. The contractor was H.H. Ackemere of Auburn. The new city hall was a handsome building with a bell tower that was used in case of fire. It also housed the Auburn Fire Department and included living space for full-time firemen. The first motorized fire truck was purchased in 1917, eliminating the need for stables for the horses.

In 1919, the Auburn Commercial Club built the building at the northeast corner of East Eighth and South Cedar Streets for its headquarters. It rented space on the ground floor for offices, including the Auburn Post Office, and reserved the second floor for its offices. A large banquet area on the lower level was the site of many meetings and dinners. The Auburn Commercial Club building was sold in the early 1960s.

As Auburn rapidly grew, the high school became inadequate, so a new school was planned. William H. McIntosh owned a large brick home on South Main Street, along with several lots. He offered his property as a site for the new school. McIntosh had been the superintendent of the Auburn Academy, county superintendent, and long a friend of education in DeKalb County. His gift was accepted and the old house was torn down to make room for the new McIntosh High School. The first brick was laid by McIntosh on July 2, 1916. Because construction was slowed by World War I, the building was not dedicated until April 18, 1921, with McIntosh also laying the last brick.

The school was a model, modern school. The gymnasium and auditorium with its gallery and stage were to save the school substantial money in rent for outside buildings for basketball games and entertainment. The ground floor housed four

EAST SIDE OF SQUARE. *The Auburn Commercial Club building, the DeKalb County Jail, and the Auburn City Hall line the east side of Cedar Street. The Court Theatre is located in the north side of the Commercial Club building. The interurban tracks are in the middle of the street.*

domestic science and vocational training rooms. The assembly room on the first floor was large enough for the entire student body. There were separate recitation rooms for each class and special rooms on the top floor for the physics, chemistry, and commercial departments. A power plant with a large round smokestack provided heat.

Alumni Gym was opened December 5, 1924. It seated 2,300 people and was the site of many "barn burner" basketball games. The gym was the home of the Auburn Red Devils, who frequently dominated area athletics and went to the Indiana State Basketball Tournament Finals in 1949.

The Auburn Commercial Club adopted the slogan "Auburn Forever with Honest Endeavor." This was sometimes abbreviated to "Auburn—City of Honest Endeavor."

Over the years, Indiana had a series of local option temperance laws, which left the question of wet or dry to the townships, towns, and cities. Any of those governmental units could elect to become dry by a majority vote of the people. Within any county, there could be both wet and dry townships and wet and dry cities or towns.

The Women's Christian Temperance Union (WCTU) has been active in DeKalb County since shortly after the national organization was founded in Cleveland in 1873. There were unions active in Auburn, Garrett, Corunna,

MOONSHINE. Sheriff's deputies pose with a still and paraphernalia from a raid. Many "speakeasies" in Auburn and Dekalb County were in the basements of private homes.

Waterloo, and Butler, which placed the WCTU Fountain on the square in the 1890s. The fountain was removed when the present courthouse was built.

The Anti-Saloon League was also active in DeKalb County. The efforts of these organizations caused almost all townships and towns to be voted dry in 1911, resulting in 11 saloons being permanently closed.

Charles Eckhart, founder of the Auburn Automobile Company, was a leading Prohibitionist in the state of Indiana and ran for Congress and for governor on the Prohibition ticket. He was politically unsuccessful, but his views prevailed in many local arenas.

The national movements of the WCTU, Anti-Saloon League, and the Prohibition Party were instrumental in securing the passage of the 18th Amendment in 1918. This amendment was ratified in 1919 and implemented in 1920. Until it was repealed by the 21st amendment, which was implemented in 1933, the nation and Auburn were dry. This led to considerable bootlegging and rum-running both nationally and locally. There were speakeasies in Auburn at several locations.

Prohibition ended quietly in 1933 and the Indiana General Assembly has regulated the liquor traffic since. In DeKalb County, local political leaders from both parties formed a company to distribute beer so they would share the function and profits, no matter which party was in power. This company, DeKalb Distributing Company, is located in Auburn at 1102 South Indiana Avenue.

In 1919, the Eckhart family sold the Auburn Automobile Company to a group of Chicago investors headed by William Wrigley Jr. The Auburn Beauty-Six was introduced the same year. This new design perked up the line for a while, but sales continued to decline. By 1924, Auburn was producing only 6 units per day and over 700 unsold touring cars filled the storage lot.

The Chicago investors, recognizing that the value of their investment in Auburn was diminishing, began looking for new blood to guide the company. Their selection was Errett Lobban Cord. Cord had made and lost $50,000 three times in California, but had recently been the aggressive sales manager of the Moon Automobile Agency in Chicago, through which he had acquired a nest egg of $100,000.

Cord became general manager of Auburn in 1924, working without salary, with the agreement that, if he turned the company around, he could acquire a controlling interest. When he got to Auburn, he ordered the stagnant inventory repainted in flashy colors and had trim and accessories added to give them a more pleasing look. The inventory was soon liquidated and E.L. Cord was headed for a spectacular career.

In 1925, Cord introduced eight-cylinder cars. Two-tone color schemes and a stylish belt line increased the appeal of the cars. Sales increased rapidly and, in 1926, Cord became president of the company. The town had a good base of industry and willing workers with an excellent work ethic. Auburn was ripe for another surge of economic activity.

AUBURN EXPORT. Auburn and Cord automobiles were exported to nearly every continent. Cars were fully crated, loaded on a railroad car, shipped to a port, and then taken to their ultimate destinations. Here, a large crane lifts a crated automobile onto a Vandalia Railroad car.

7. Fiery Crosses, FWD, and V12s: The Roaring Twenties (1926–1932)

Gradual changes in Grover's Corners. Horses are getting rarer. Farmers coming into town in Fords. Everybody locks their house doors now at night. Ain't been any burglars in town yet, but everybody's heard about 'em.

~Thorton Wilder, *Our Town*

The phenomenal success of E.L. Cord could not have been predicted. The Auburn Automobile Company gave him the platform he needed to work his magic on the economy and financial markets. Within four years, he had purchased or controlled 64 companies. Some say that he used our town. Others would argue that he brought Auburn back and that the heritage he left has kept Auburn on the map.

Transportation was enhanced with the establishment of the Auburn Airport in 1927, while the interurban system declined.

The dark side of our town came forth in white robes in the form of the Ku Klux Klan. Many would like to forget that the Ku Klux Klan was once a powerful force in Auburn and DeKalb County. This was indeed a dark chapter in our history, but lest we are too hard on our ancestors, we must understand the KKK in its context of the 1920s.

The Ku Klux Klan was very active in Auburn and DeKalb County in the early and mid-1920s. The records of the DeKalb County Klan's secretary, or Kligrajzs, as he was called, indicated that as many as 2,500 DeKalb County men were members between 1924 and 1926. This total is probably larger than any other single organization in the county before or since.

The original Ku Klux Klan was organized in the South in 1865 by Civil War veterans. It was then perverted into an instrument of terrorism of African Americans. This organization grew rapidly, did a lot of damage in the South, but was dead by 1872.

The twentieth-century Ku Klux Klan owed many of its principles to Know-Nothingism and its name, regalia, and some of its outlandish terminology to the Reconstruction Klan. The later Klan organization was founded in Georgia

AUBURN AUTOMOBILE COMPANY. This aerial view shows most of the 26 buildings of the Auburn Automobile Company. The present Auburn Cord Duesenberg Museum and National Automotive and Truck Museum (NATMUS) are in the foreground.

by Colonel William J. Simmons, but did not progress until Hiram Wesley Evans, a Dallas dentist, took over and became its Imperial Wizard. Under Evans's leadership, the Klan membership rose to six million in 1924, the high-water mark of the Invisible Empire.

Indiana represented a cross-section of the United States and was fertile ground for the Klan. If Indiana was a microcosm of the United States, DeKalb County was a microcosm of Indiana.

The basic old-line families, landowners, and merchants were conservative second or third generation people of English and German backgrounds. The growth of the railroads and industry in DeKalb County had brought many recent immigrants into the county. These people were welcomed and accepted during the time of an expanding economy, such as the period from 1900 to 1915. Indeed, these people were necessary labor for the established population. During and after World War I, there was a different atmosphere. The economy was not so good. A general mood of intolerance developed and became widespread. There was generally a resentment of anyone perceived to be "foreign" whether they were Catholic, Jewish, African American, recent immigrants, or just a bit different.

By 1920, the postwar scramble for jobs was intense. Hoosiers did not like competing with foreigners for jobs that they thought should rightfully be theirs. In this atmosphere, any organization sworn to uphold hearth, firesides, womanly virtue, Americanism, patriotism, and law and order was welcomed with open arms. In actuality, the Klan waged "righteous" war on Bolsheviks, Catholics, Jews, African Americans, bootleggers, pacifists, evolutionists, foreigners, and particularly on any and all persons whom they deemed "immoral." The Klan's Declaration of Principles stated its general purpose as follows:

> We proclaim to the world that we are dedicated to the sublime duty of providing generous aid, tender sympathy and fraternal assistance amid fortune and misfortune in the effulgent light of life and amid the sable shadows of death; and to the exalted privilege of demonstrating the practical utility of the great (yet most neglected), doctrine of the Fatherhood of God and the Brotherhood of man as a vital force in the lives and affairs of men. We invite all men who can qualify to become citizens of the Invisible Empire to approach the portal of our beneficent domain join us in our noble work of extending its boundaries, and in disseminating the gospel of "Klankraft" thereby encouraging, conserving, protecting and making vital the fraternal relationship in the practice of an honorable clannishness to share with us the glory of performing the sacred duty of protecting womanhood; to maintain forever the God given supremacy of the white race; to commemorate the holy and

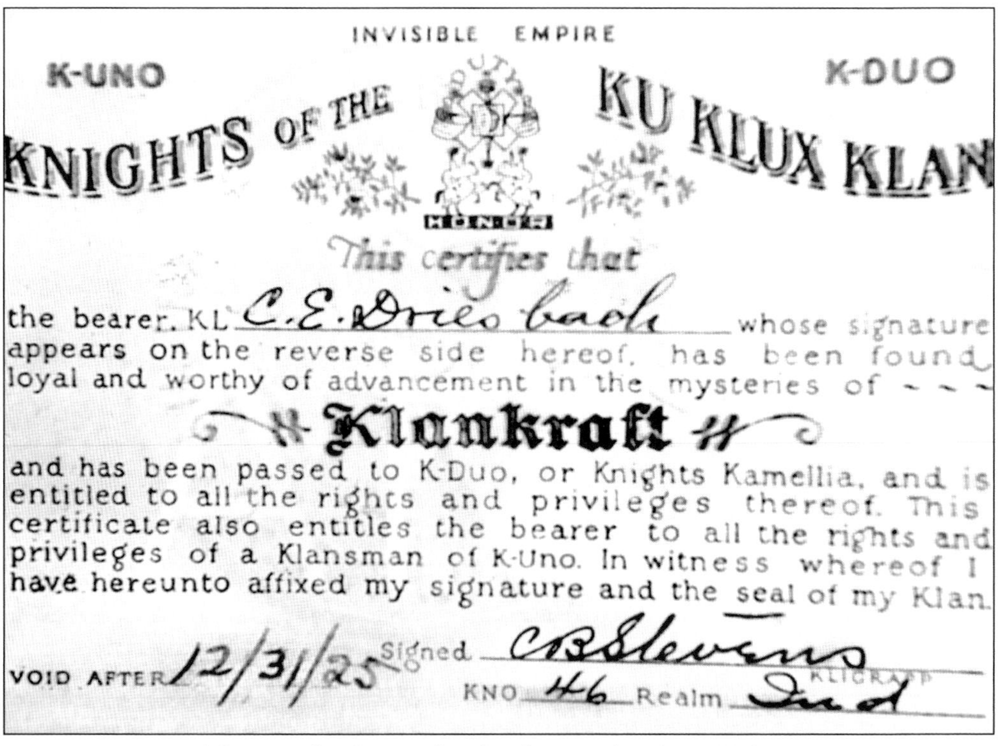
INVISIBLE EMPIRE

K-UNO K-DUO

KNIGHTS OF THE KU KLUX KLAN

This certifies that

the bearer. KL C. E. Driesbach whose signature appears on the reverse side hereof, has been found loyal and worthy of advancement in the mysteries of

Klankraft

and has been passed to K-Duo, or Knights Kamellia, and is entitled to all the rights and privileges thereof. This certificate also entitles the bearer to all the rights and privileges of a Klansman of K-Uno. In witness whereof I have hereunto affixed my signature and the seal of my Klan.

VOID AFTER 12/31/25 Signed CBStevens KLIGRAPP

KNO 46 Realm Ind

KU KLUX KLAN. This membership card is dated December 31, 1925.

> chivalric achievements or our fathers; to safeguard the sacred rights, privileges and institutions of our Civil Government; to bless mankind and to keep eternally ablaze the sacred fire of a fervent devotion to pure Americanism.
>
> The Invisible Empire is founded on sterling character, and immutable principles based upon sacred sentiment and cemented by noble purposes. It is promoted by a sincere, unselfish devotion of the souls of men, and is governed by their consecrated intelligence. It is the soul of chivalry, virtue's impenetrable shield; and the devout impulse of an unconquered race.

D.C. Stephenson was to become the impetus of the Invisible Empire in Indiana and a number of other northern states. He started organizing the Indiana Klan in Evansville in 1922, moved to Columbus, Ohio, and ended up in Indianapolis as his part of the empire grew. Soon, 20 other states from Maine to Nebraska came under his control.

Recruiting Klan members was an easy task. The principles were as conservative as some of those being espoused today and as imbedded in Christian tradition as those of Jerry Falwell's Moral Majority. The pyramid sales methods were as sophisticated and slick as those of Am-Way. Indeed, the most prolific organizers were Protestant clergymen, particularly those of the Methodist Episcopal persuasion.

Klan memberships were sold for $10 each, of which D.C. Stephenson received $4. The balance was split by others up and down the pyramid. The white robes and peaked hats cost $1.10 each, but were sold for $5 to $10 each. It was estimated that D.C. Stephenson made between $2 million and $5 million in 18 months. Full-time organizers, many of them former salesmen in Florida real estate promotions, fanned out across the states.

The "abracadabra" common to secret orders appealed to Hoosiers, who were well versed in the ways and customs of lodges from the Masons to the Odd Fellows. Individual Klaverns met weekly. Many of their meetings were no more than poker or euchre sessions in club rooms. The Auburn club rooms were located at 408 South Main Street, above the John Hursh grocery store.

From time to time, posters would appear announcing a Konklave, which was a meeting in a public place with a cross burning, or a Klavalcade, which was a parade of members in full regalia. At the appointed time, usually about dusk, the robed and hooded Klansmen quietly gathered at the appointed place and proceeded with the business at hand.

In Auburn, outdoor meetings were held in Larry Brandon's woods on the north edge of town. On June 15, 1923, the DeKalb County Ku Klux Klan officers were elected in an open air meeting on the north side of Auburn. There were 2,200 members in the county, with 700 of those from Auburn.

The regalia for the DeKalb County Klan is still extant. It includes separate robes and masks for each officer. While the robes and masks are primarily white, they have various colored emblems and piping, which designate positions. There also were full white covers for horses. Saplings were cut from the woods to make a cross. These were usually transported in an open car to the site, doused with kerosene, and then lit.

Only one local instance has been related involving an African American. A merchant at Waterloo hired a black man to assist in his business. The Klan believed that he and the merchant's wife were having an affair and burned a cross in front of the couple's house. The man soon left town, and the couple subsequently divorced.

Most crosses were reserved for philandering husbands. First, a "Fiery Summons," with the alleged act set forth in red ink, was posted on the husband's door, car, or toolbox at work. If he mended his ways, nothing further happened. If he did not, a cross would be burned for all to see. This usually resulted in an improvement of his conduct. If not, more drastic action would be taken, such as a clandestine beating or damage to his property or car.

Thus, the Klan was the strong-arm self-appointed monitor of morals in Auburn and DeKalb County. Their power reached a peak in the period from 1924 to 1926. D.C. Stephenson assumed the title of Grand Dragon of the Realm of Indiana. On July 4, 1923, he arranged the largest Konklave ever held in Indiana. Over 200,000 knights assembled in a huge field near Kokomo whereupon Stephenson swooped down from the sky in a gilded airplane. He appeared clad in resplendent robes, pledged his unfaltering leadership, and then departed majestically while the hysterical mob threw coins and jewelry at him.

Stephenson called himself the foremost mass psychologist of all time. His ambition was to become President of the United States. He targeted the Senate seat of Sam Ralston in 1924 and the 1928 presidential nomination. The Klan did not affiliate exclusively with one party, but elected its members and supporters regardless of party. In DeKalb County, several Democratic leaders and party members were Klan supporters. Most often though, the Klan gained power by using the Republican party, probably because the Republicans were already in control of Indiana, so Stephenson affiliated with them on a statewide basis.

In the 1924 primary election, the Klan supported Ed Jackson, a Republican candidate for governor. He handily won with Klan support. There followed a rift between D.C. Stephenson and the National Klan organization. H.W. Evans, the Imperial Wizard, charged Stephenson with "conduct unbecoming a Klansman" involving a manicurist and ordered Stephenson's home Klavern at Evansville to try him.

Stephenson summoned Klansmen from all Indiana counties to Cadle Tabernacle in Indianapolis where he succeeded in severing the Indiana Klan from the National Klan to avoid his trial by the Evansville Klavern. While the vote was clearly in his favor, this event began a split in the Klan. For many years, criminal prosecutions had been common in Indiana politics. During its short tenure, the Klan had been masters of using this technique for political control and harassment. Now Stephenson claimed this technique was being used against him when, on March 25, 1925, a woman who claimed to be his first wife from long ago, came to Indianapolis at the expense of rival Klansmen and sued him for desertion and nonsupport.

Stephenson did not need too much help from his adversaries, however, to plot the path to his downfall. On April 2, 1925, D.C. Stephenson was charged and arrested for the murder of Madge Oberholtzer. Less than a year earlier, he had won political control of the state and declared, "I am the law of Indiana." Now he was charged with the murder of a young woman under circumstances that involved the grossest violations of moral turpitude. What an ironic twist for the leader of an organization sworn to uphold virtue and morality! Stephenson's actions are a classic example of the adage that "power corrupts and absolute power corrupts absolutely."

Madge Oberholtzer was an Indianapolis secretary who was acquainted with Stephenson. He induced or forced her to take an overnight trip with him on the Monon Railroad to Hammond. The two shared a compartment on the train. Stephenson sexually assaulted and mutilated her. They ended up in a hotel in Hammond. Madge was so mortified and embarrassed by what had happened to her that she secretly left the hotel room and went to a drugstore where she purchased a poisonous substance. She went back to the hotel and ingested the poison. She became very ill and was soon discovered by Stephenson and his cronies. Rather than seeking medical attention for her, they took her back to

GARRETT COLORED GIANTS. There were few African Americans in Dekalb County. Those who did reside in the county lived in Garrett, at least enough to field a baseball team. In this era, black teams could only play other black teams.

MOON TRUCKING COMPANY. The Silver Moon Toy Company made wheeled toys from wood. The horse's front legs were articulated to make it look like the horse was walking when a child pushed the toy across the floor

Indianapolis on the next train and delivered her to her parents' home. Her parents sought medical help, but she lived for only 12 days.

Oberholtzer made an elaborate "dying declaration" of what had happened to her. Though Stephenson had no direct hand in her death, he was charged, tried, and convicted of murder. The case still stands as a textbook example of the least causation in an American case resulting in a conviction for murder.

The downfall of D.C. Stephenson resulted in the rapid decline of the Klan in Indiana. Local Klan members feared they would in some way become implicated in Stephenon's case if they continued their Klan membership. The decline of the Klan was almost as rapid as its rise. By 1928, it was no longer a force in Indiana. The DeKalb County Klavern was finally disbanded in 1935 and the regalia and records moved to the home of the secretary.

This generation should probably not be too critical of ancestors who may have been members of the DeKalb County Klavern. They were more probably victims of the grandiose scheme of D.C. Stephenson, rather than willing and informed devotees. It is probably fortunate that Stephenson's sexual appetite broke his rise to power. One could speculate that his doctrines and methods could have resulted in an American Hitler. There were surely intriguing similarities and ambitions.

Organizations of greater worth and longevity were chartered in Auburn in 1928. The Auburn Lions Club has accomplished many civic projects through the years. Likewise the Auburn Rotary Club has been of great benefit to the community.

While the stock market crashed on October 29, 1929, the Depression did not hit Auburn until several years later. Generally, Auburn's ultra-conservative banks and industries were well capitalized and traditionally maintained large resources of cash.

Indeed, several new industries were founded in this era. The Auburn Burner Company was founded in 1931 by J.D. Casey and his son-in-law Harry C. McIntyre to manufacture oil burners whereby an existing coal furnace could be converted to burn fuel oil. There was some advantage to burning fuel oil, in that the messy, dusty, dirty coal could be eliminated, as could the uncertainty of the supply of coal at the whim of coal miners' unions and railroad unions.

Foley Pattern Company was founded in 1930 by George L. Foley to make wood and metal patterns for the cast metal industries, which would have included the Auburn Foundry.

The Sterlite Foundry and Manufacturing Company was founded in the early 1930s to manufacture various products from an alloy known as Sterlite, a form of stainless steel. This company was located in the former McIntyre factory at 104 Walnut Street. Charles W. Rachel, Aubrey L. Kuhlman, and Raymond Sliteler were the local principals.

Silver Moon Toy Company was an enterprise of Rollie H. Muhn during the early 1930s. Muhn's construction company shops were located just south of the Silver Moon Dance Hall, formerly located at 3276–3286–3296 County Road 427, and were used by the Silver Moon Toy Company to manufacture a line of wooden toys. The line included such items as walking cats and ducks, oxen and carts, horses, and milk delivery wagons. The toys were colorfully lacquered. Freight was shipped on the interurban line that ran adjacent to the site. Offices were also located at 924 East Seventh Street.

The dominant industry of Auburn was the Auburn Automobile Company. E.L. Cord, despite his young age and lack of direct experience, was a financial genius. He considered the Great Depression an opportunity. In 1927, Cord convinced the Auburn Automobile Company to race Auburn Automobiles and, in July, the cars broke all speed records for stock cars from 5 to 5,000 miles at the Atlantic City Speedway.

In 1928, Alan Leamy was hired as a stylist and the fabulous boat-tailed Auburn speedster was introduced. Wade Morton drove an Auburn 8-115 Speedster 108.46 miles per hour over a measured mile at Daytona, drove 2,033 miles in 24 hours for a record of 84.7 miles per hour at the Atlantic City Speedway, and set a new record at Pikes Peak.

Most Auburn dealers had been small independent garages throughout the country. Cord began building a network of full line dealers that helped sales considerably. An export division headed by R.S. Wiley resulted in many cars being shipped throughout the world.

In 1929, Cord began to acquire other companies to add to his growing empire. He purchased Ansted Engine Company, Lexington Motor Car Company, Lycoming Engine Company, Limousine Body Company, and Duesenberg Motors. The Central Manufacturing company included many manufacturing buildings and land in Connersville, Indiana.

The Leamy-designed aerodynamic Auburn Cabin Speedster was the sensation of the New York Automobile Show in 1929. The car was based largely on airplane design factors and was truly revolutionary.

The Cord L-29 was also introduced in 1929. It caught the automotive world by surprise and was widely acclaimed, but was never a commercial success. The L-29 Cord was built from 1929 to 1931 (157 leftover models were titled in 1932). These were outstanding automobiles and have a special place in American automotive history.

The L-29 Cord was the first production front-wheel-drive car in the United States. The L-29 was introduced to fill the gap between the low priced Auburn and the top-of-the-line Duesenberg in the Cord Corporation line of cars. The front-wheel-drive Ruxton was also introduced in 1929. The technology for front-wheel-drive had been available for some time, but it was not until it was used in Indianapolis 500 racecars that it was deemed practical for a production car.

Herb Snow was the chief engineer and was responsible for the revolutionary features, including an X-frame bracing concept and, of course, the front-wheel-drive

ERRETT LOBBAN CORD. Cord was pictured on the cover of the January 18, 1932 issue of Time *magazine. The article on the automobile industry lauded Cord for Auburn's success despite the Great Depression. It stated, "The U.S. was on the downside of the Depression, yet here was an automobile at $945.00 with racy lines. It looked rich and would do 80 miles per hour. It answered the need of many a man who had lost his shirt but hoped his friends did not know it. It made many another man who never had it to lose, feel like a million dollars."*

L-29 CORD. An L-29 Cord Convertible Sedan is photographed outside of a factory building. The L-29 was the first production front-wheel-drive (FWD) automobile in the United States.

unit. The car seemed expensive, but was really underpriced considering its features. The sedan and brougham were $3,095, and the cabriolet and phaeton were $3,295. Alan Leamy was the stylist. He created a lovely, low-silhouette car that is today considered one of the most outstanding designs of the era.

Only 5,010 L-29s were built over the three years that it was in production. Despite its price being lowered to $2,395, the car could not survive. The Cord was re-introduced in 1936.

The Depression had little effect on the cash-flushed company. The L-29/ Experimental Building (now National Automotive and Truck Museum of the United States) was built in 1928. The Administration Building (now Auburn Cord Duesenberg Museum) was built in 1930 to house the Cord Corporation, which had been established as a holding company for the ever-expanding Cord interests. In 1932, a 12-cylinder engine was offered in an Auburn costing less than $1,000. This automobile broke additional speed and endurance records.

E.L. Cord built the house at 368 West Seventh Street when he came to town in 1924. Several years later, he built the house at 1000 North Main Street, a location that was contiguous to his Auburn Airport to the west. He married his first wife, Helen Marie Frische, at Santa Ana, California on September 19, 1914. Helen died of cancer on September 13, 1930, leaving him a widower with two young sons at the age of 36.

AUBURN POSTCARD MANUFACTURING COMPANY. Located adjacent to Cedar Creek on East Seventh Street, the company supplied postcards throughout the United States.

Cord then moved the headquarters of the Cord Corporation to Chicago. Cord left Auburn for Chicago in 1932. He married Virginia Tharp on January 3, 1931 and they moved to California where they built Cord Haven, a mansion equal or superior to the mansions of the contemporary movie stars.

Cord left the day-to-day operations of the Auburn Automobile Company in the hands of a series of presidents beginning in 1930. The Cord Corporation had purchased the former buildings of the Lexington Motor Car Company on May 10, 1937, and moved much of the automobile assembly there. By 1932, only the administration, service, and experimental departments remained at Auburn, along with some parts manufacturing activities. Only the experimental and hand-built cars were built at Auburn from that time.

In 1932, the Messenger Publishing Company of Chicago purchased all assets of Auburn Greeting Card Company, formerly Auburn Postcard Company, and moved its operation to Auburn where the two companies were consolidated.

The Messenger Publishing Company was founded by Frank M. Messenger in 1913. A religious man, Messenger recognized that too few people regularly read the scriptures. He conceived the idea of publishing a calendar which presented a daily scripture as a means of conveying the gospel into millions of homes in a subtle manner. In 1914, over 100,000 calendars were printed in just seven months.

As the use of postcards declined, the Auburn Postcard Company changed its name to Auburn Greeting Card Company and published an extensive line of greeting cards, many of which had a religious theme.

The consolidation of the two companies was a good mix. The art department remained in Chicago, but production was in Auburn. The company added a line of printing for funeral directors, including acknowledgment folders, memorial service folders, prayer cards, mass cards, and register books. The calendars were offered to the general public via advertising placed in national publications such as *McCalls*, *Ladies Home Journal*, *Good Housekeeping*, *Woman's Home Companion*, and *Christian Herald*. Later calendars were imprinted with the name of churches and "compliments" of a local funeral home and then distributed free to church members, providing an effective, yet subtle, means of placing the name of a funeral home before the public in a form of religious scripture calendar which they presumably looked at daily.

The most prevalent image of Christ painted by Walter Sallman was used for many years by Messenger and led to the image being nearly universally accepted as *the* image of Christ. It can bc said that Auburn's Messenger Corporation was responsible for disseminating this image throughout the world!

The company was sensitive to the doctrine of many religions and published special calendars for Catholics, Lutherans, Episcopals, Jews, and Latter Day Saints. Calendars and other publications were also published in French, Polish, Spanish, Greek, and Italian. Messenger had staff artists who did much of the artwork for cards and calendars. Noted artists with a national reputation were also used on a contract basis.

While many of Messenger's products were of a fleeting, ephemeral nature, they put the Auburn name and mark of usefulness and quality in millions of homes throughout the United States and many foreign countries.

One of Auburn's esteemed citizens of this era was Frank Carlton Nelson, Auburn's own Poet Laureate. He published two small volumes entitled *Along Life's Road* (1927) and *The Evening Hour* (1934), but was always available to write a poem for a special event such as a marriage or an anniversary. He remembered his roots in *My Old Home Town*:

I have never longed for honors great,
For wealth I have never yearned,
A titled name is a thing I hate,
When I know that it isn't earned.
I have no wish for great renown,
But this I'd love to be—
Just half as good to my old home town,
As my home town is to me.

The little boosts and the words of praise
From my neighbors staunch and true,
Their little helps in a thousand ways,
And the kindly things they do.
The pleasant smile and the glad "Hello"
When I feel that my hopes are down,
Are but a part of the debt I owe
To the folks of my old home town.

It's "Howdy Bill" and "Howdy Joe"
 And "How are the folks today?"
It's meeting friends that I'm proud to know,
 That cheers me on my way.
I've traveled east and I've traveled west,
 I have been from sea to sea,
But my old home town I love the best,
 For my home town's best to me.

So, this my prayer, as the years go by,
 To the Master up above,
Just let me live and let me die,
 In the little town I love.
May I do the things that I ought to do,
 May I be what I ought to be,
To my old home town may I be as true
 As my home town is to me.

SCENE IN ECKHART PARK. The Eckhart family established Eckhart Park to accommodate automobile travelers. The dam provided a "swimming hole" for Auburn kids.

8. Coffin Noses and Headed South: The Great Depression (1933–1939)

Happiness lies not in the mere possession of money; it lies in the joy of achievement, in the thrill of creative effort. The joy and moral stimulation of work no longer must be forgotten in the mad chase of evanescent profits. These dark days will be worth all they cost us if they teach us that our true destiny is not to be ministered unto but to minister to ourselves and to fellow men.

~Franklin Delano Roosevelt, First Inaugural Address, March 4, 1933

Auburn resident and former president of the Auburn Automobile Company James I. Farley joined President Roosevelt in Washington as a congressman in the 73rd Congress. A Democrat, he served until 1939. He died in 1941 and is interred at Woodlawn Cemetery.

The Auburn Automobile Company had its best year in 1931 when it sold 34,045 automobiles with gross sales of $37,224,092 and when it ranked eighth among all car companies. The 1934 models designed by Alan Leamy were a commercial failure in the marketplace. It is not clear whether this was because of the design or because of the deepening effects of the Depression.

Gordon M. Buehrig, a young designer at Duesenberg, was brought to Auburn to re-design the car. Alan Leamy left Auburn for employment with Ford, but soon died as a result of an inoculation administered in preparation for a trip to Europe.

Working with two draftsmen, Buehrig revamped the basic Auburn with a different grille and hood and designed the fabulous Auburn Speedster in a period of six weeks. The new models were brought out in August and were well received, but sales were disappointing.

Despite the Depression, the decline in cash reserves, and the disappointing sales of the Auburn, the company began designing and engineering a new model Cord to be known as the 810. Buehrig was given a nearly free hand, but a limited budget. He designed one of the most revolutionary cars ever produced by an American automobile manufacturer. His limited budget forced him to achieve some unusual production techniques, including interchangeable doors and a unibody concept with the engine and front-wheel-drive system. Other features included disappearing headlights, concealed gas cap, no running boards, and an electric shifting mechanism. While some thought that the "new Cord" was part of a scheme by E.L. Cord to drive up the price of Cord Corporation stock, the re-designed Cord was a truly revolutionary automobile ahead of its time.

The rules of the New York Automobile Show required that at least 100 cars were to have been built prior to January 1, 1936, to be eligible to exhibit at the show. Therefore, the first 100 cars were hand-built in the Experimental Building (now National Automotive and Truck Museum) while state of the art manufacturing facilities were being readied at Connersville. The 810 Cord was the hit of the New York Automobile Show, with hundreds of orders taken.

Although the stock market crashed on October 29, 1929, the Great Depression did not hit Auburn until about 1934 because of the continued success of the Auburn Automobile Company in the interim. Gradually, the effects of the Depression were felt in Auburn. The new Cord was produced in Connersville. Only the administration, parts, factory service, and experimental departments remained at Auburn. Several workers commuted to Connersville for continuing employment with the company.

The Auburn Automobile Company was in the hands of Harold Ames as president after 1932. E.L. Cord had moved on to bigger and better things and seemed to have lost interest in the company that had enabled him to leverage his talent into a mega-corporation worth millions of dollars. He did, however, have direct input into the design and production of the 810 Cord.

While the new Cord was engineered and designed in Auburn, it was to be produced at Connersville in a new facility with state-of-the-art production techniques, including automatic electric welding machines for the all-steel bodies. (Most cars prior to this time had a wood body frame covered with a sheet-metal skin.)

Cord's empire continued to grow. The Depression was an opportunity for him to acquire additional companies. He had the vision to foresee what industries would be emerging and which would be declining in the marketplace. He was particularly interested in air travel. He owned, via Cord Corporation, Stinson Aircraft Company, Lycoming Engine Company, Colonial Airlines, and over 20 other aircraft manufacturers or carriers.

In an interview with a reporter for the *Kansas City Star* in 1933, he said, "I'm tired of hearing about the depression. It's another incident in the world's economic history. The World goes on. Intelligent men profit by history. The intelligent young man reads back, then looks forward."

Cord learned to fly under the tutelage of Big Wild Bill Fitzsimmons at the Auburn Airport. He flew his own Stinson and, after moving to California, he often flew from coast to coast. His influence on the stock market was so profound that the *New York Times* often reported when he had left California and headed for New York. Before the Securities and Exchange Commission was established, Cord could manipulate the financial market at will with the help of his staff. He appeared on the cover of *Time* magazine twice.

Due to charges filed against him by the United States Security and Exchange Commission in 1937, Cord divested himself of Cord Corporation Stock. The new leaders of Cord Corporation did not favor the production of automobiles and ordered production of the Cord ceased.

It was a sad day in 1937 when the Auburn Automobile Company filed bankruptcy. E.L. Cord's interest had been held through the Cord Corporation, which had gradually divested itself of much of the stock. The bankruptcy of Auburn Automobile Company was just a blip on the financial scope of the Cord Corporation.

The bankruptcy was filed in the United States District Court in Fort Wayne. The records of the bankruptcy are a part of the Tri Kappa Collection of Automotive Literature at the Auburn Cord Duesenberg Museum and contain about 5,000 pages providing a "snapshot" in time of the company at the time of its demise.

The assets were liquidated. Fortunately for the city of Auburn, most of the Auburn Automobile Company real estate, except for the Administration Building, was sold to Warner Automotive Parts Division of Borg-Warner Corporation, which moved its production of "after market" parts to Auburn. This proved to be a good basic industry for Auburn because during the Depression and then into the war years, people kept their older cars running and serviceable by the use of after-market parts. Those employees, such as Lester See, who were retained to liquidate the Auburn Automobile Company, were then hired by Borg-Warner.

CORDS AT THE INDIANAPOLIS 500 RACE. 1936 Cord 810s were used by race officials at the Indianapolis 500.

ARCOR PRODUCTS. The Auburn Rubber Company had an elaborate display in the industrial tent of the DeKalb County Free Fall Fair. Auburn Safe Play Toys were advertised in many national magazines.

See reported that he never missed a day's work: "My last day for Auburn was April 8, 1938. The next day I started working for Borg-Warner, a job which I continued until I retired in 1972."

Borg-Warner moved many employees to Auburn from its plant in Muncie. Those employees became good citizens of Auburn. Many became community leaders, including Mayor Don Allison.

The administration building was sold to Dallas Winslow, who was in the business of purchasing parts from defunct automobile companies. Winslow continued to make parts available for as long as there was demand for them. He purchased the supply of parts for Auburn, Cord, and Duesenberg and then consolidated at Auburn the parts supply of the other companies that he had acquired, including Graham, Hupmobile, Star, Durant, and Rugby cars and trucks.

What if the Auburn Automobile Company had survived? What would Auburn have been like? This question has often been pondered by residents of the City of Auburn.

Lest it appear that the Auburn Automobile Company and its demise was all that happened in this era, mention should be made of three other industries—one new to Auburn and two existing.

The Atwood Vacuum Machine Company originated in 1936 at Rockford, Illinois. The owners, Seth B. Atwood and James T. Atwood, acquired the right to several clutch designs invented by C.A. and W.V. Thelander in 1932. W.V. Thelander was taken into the Atwood organization to establish a laboratory set up in Rockford for further testing and development. The purpose was to complete the designs and have them ready for sale to the automotive and tractor trade.

In October 1937, the Atwoods purchased the former Sterlite Plant on Lincoln Street between Wayne and South Van Buren Streets, and established the Auburn Manufacturing Company to manufacture Thelander Clutches. Production started in January 1939.

The clutch line consisted of the "Auburn" spring-loaded design, vibration damper discs, and the "constant pressure" line of clutches. By 1940, the customer list had grown to several tractor manufacturers, two earth-moving manufacturers, and one automotive manufacturer. This industry filled some of the void caused by the demise of the Auburn Automobile Company.

The Auburn Foundry had developed a line of stokers in 1921 that came to be known as the "Auburn Stoker." In 1936, it developed a line of mechanical worm feed stokers for domestic, household applications. Most houses of this era were heated with coal that was delivered to a coal bin in the basement. From there the residents had to keep the furnace filled with coal about every six hours. The last chore prior to retiring at night was to "tend the fire" and the first chore upon rising was to stoke the fire again. By morning, the fire was usually reduced to embers and the house had become quite cold.

A worm feed stoker using coal in small lumps could be placed into a large hopper and then fed by a "worm" into the furnace as the thermostat called for more heat. This device enabled the furnace to be left untended for two to three days, a great advantage to homeowners.

The Auburn Rubber Company had manufactured tires and industrial rubber products since its founding as the Double Fabric Tire Company in 1913. In 1935, it began to make toys out of rubber.

The principal stockholder, A.L. Murray, had been to England and brought back a Palace Guard toy soldier made out of lead. He thought that toy soldiers could be made out of rubber and had his pattern makers make molds from the lead guard. Rubber samples were made and then decorated by Edward McCandlish, a freelance artist. The samples were presented to toy buyers and the toys immediately caught on.

The first Auburn rubber soldiers were molded in 24-inch rubber presses, each of which contained 40 to 60 soldiers. The soldiers were then trimmed, dipped into a base-color lacquer, and sent down a conveyor where as many as 24 women using camel hair brushes painted on the details of faces, shoes, belts, buttons, medals, and eyes. When dry, each soldier was wrapped in waxed paper and packed three dozen to a carton. Figures of baseball and football teams were also made at an early date. The first toy automobile was a 1936 Cord. Thus began the production of wheeled toys, which was to result in millions being produced and sold throughout the country. There is probably not a person who, as a child during the 1940s, 1950s and 1960s, did not play with Auburn Rubber Toys. They predated plastics and were the inexpensive successors to metal toys. Most were sold in the dime stores of that era. Many different boxed sets were offered, including farm sets, fire sets, and construction sets.

Thus, the "Auburn" name became further known throughout the country in the form of clutches, stokers, and toys.

Chester J. Hodge was a justice of the peace for Union Township. Among the authority granted to JPs, as they were called, was the power to marry. During this era, Indiana marriage laws were much more liberal than in Michigan, Ohio, and other eastern states. A couple could come to Indiana in the morning, be married, and return home in the evening. Squire Hodge set himself up as the "Marrying Justice." His residence at 412 North Main Street was the "Marrying Parlor." He advertised "Marriages Solemnized Any Time Day or Night," that "Auburn has two good jewelry stores at which to buy engagement and wedding rings," and that "Auburn has an unusually fine hotel at which to stop."

The tranquility of the upper midwest was interrupted from time to time by the exploits of John Dillinger and his gang. After a particularly daring raid on the Lima, Ohio jail that resulted in the freedom of Dillinger, Auburn Police Chief Charles Davis announced that his department was prepared and had a more than adequate arsenal of weapons, including a Thompson submachine gun and bullet-proof vests. Dillinger may have learned of the chief's announcement and initiated future plans around it.

On Saturday, October 14, 1933, the Auburn arsenal was wiped out without a shot being fired. The following Monday's edition of the *Evening Star* reported:

> A group of daring bandits, believed to have been led by Walter Deitrich, who was among ten prisoners at Michigan City who escaped recently, and Harry Copeland, a paroled convict, made a raid on the police station at the Auburn City Hall Saturday night, held up two officers and made away with about one thousand dollars worth of weapons and ammunition, including a machine gun.
>
> A wide search is underway for the desperadoes, but so far without avail. Two veteran members of the police force, Fred Krueger and Henry West, were the victims of the outlaws. They were threatened with guns in their ribs, but were not harmed. The hold-up required only a few minutes' time and the loot consisted of a Thompson machine gun, a common .38 caliber revolver, a .38 Smith and Wesson revolver, a .30 caliber Springfield Army rifle, a 401 Winchester automatic rifle, a .45 caliber Colt's revolver, a .44 special Smith and Wesson revolver, a .25 Spanish Automatic pistol, a .38 German Luger revolver, a large quantity of ammunition and three bullet proof vests.
>
> The police office is located in the front of the building, which is situated at Ninth and Cedar Streets, opposite the Court House. In

NATIONAL 5 & 10¢ STORE COMPANY. This store was located on South Main Street between Eighth and Ninth Streets. For 1¢, the machine in front printed a ticket stating one's weight and fortune.

one corner of the room is a desk where Officer West was sitting when Officer Krueger entered at 11:20 o'clock carrying a sack of popcorn. Mr. Krueger sat down, his back towards the door. Immediately thereafter, two well dressed men about thirty years old strode into the room, each brandishing two revolvers, one in each hand.

Walking up to Officer West, one of them said, "You might as well sit still. We don't want to kill anyone unless we have to. Have you got any guns?" Mr. Krueger stood up and answered "Yes" at the same time reaching towards his hip pocket. "Oh, no" said Krueger as the bandit reached into the officer's pocket and removed the revolver. Mr. West was forced to surrender the gun he was carrying in like manner. One of the bandits then commanded the officers to furnish a key to the gun cabinet located beside the desk. The officers started to demur, but with guns in close proximity to their ribs, Mr. West produced a key and unlocked the cabinet.

Mr. Krueger in the meantime had glanced out the window in an effort to get a look at the bandit's automobile. He failed to see it, but one of the hoodlums thereupon ordered him to face the opposite wall. After removing a few of the guns from the cabinet, one of the bandits remarked, "Why not put these fellows into a cell and get rid of them?"

Suiting the action to the word the bandits forced Mr. Krueger to get a key to a cell from a desk and the officers were then marched into a cell, which is just in the rear of the office, and locked them up. In doing so, one of the bandits remarked to Mr. Krueger, "I have heard of you for thirty years."

The outlaws were heard making two trips after the loot. The officers got a glance at a third man who was in the hall evidently posted to handle any visitors to the City Hall. It presumed the bandits' automobile was nearby. After they made their departure the officers called across Ninth Street to George Anderson. He hurried to the City Hall and got another key from the desk. He released the officers and an alarm was given, but no trace of the bandits could be found.

The machine gun and vests were the property of the City and the .25 caliber pistol belonged to the Chief of Police Charles Davis, but the other weapons and most of the ammunition were owned by officers West and Krueger.

Sheriff John P. Hoff and Chief of Police Davis left the City Hall only a few minutes before the raid. As soon as they learned of the crime they spread the word to surrounding counties and to state police headquarters. It was deemed probable that not only Deitrich and Copeland were implicated, but also John Dillinger, who was freed from Allen County [Ohio] jail last week after killing the Sheriff.

AUBURN CITY HALL. The jail is to the left and the fire department is to the right. John Dillinger's gang came through the front entrance.

It was reported that, sometime after the weapon robbery, Auburn Mayor Warren Lige received a letter from Dillinger stating that he appreciated his bullet-proof vests, but that one of them had proved unsatisfactory—the guy wearing it had been killed in Hammond during a bank robbery.

The Dillinger gang continued to terrorize the Midwest. Police feared they planned a wholesale attack on the Indiana State Prison with the Auburn arsenal. This fear was never realized.

Police were always on Dillinger's trail, but found it difficult to apprehend him. An embryonic state police force, with fewer than 60 officers and without two-way radios, was no match to the gang and its fast cars and well planned and well executed activities. Dillinger's bank robberies continued and his notoriety spread until he was finally shot on July 22, 1934 by police when he was leaving a Chicago theatre in the company of the "Lady in Red."

A search of his apartment after his death established that Dillinger was in fact one of the Auburn trio. Police found a map of DeKalb County showing the location of the Auburn City Hall, all DeKalb County banks, and proposed getaway routes. Three of Dillinger's gang members were from Fort Wayne—Clifford Mohler, Sam Goldstein, and Homer Van Meter.

It is difficult to visualize the terror that gang crime imposed upon the people of Indiana in the 1930s. An International News Service story of March 3, 1934 stated, "So desperate became the crime situation in Indiana that Governor Paul V. McNutt . . . ordered 640 National Guardsmen in 70 squads of nine men each to be mobilized as deputy sheriffs in an unprecedented war on the marauding convict gang . . ." Policemen and National Guardsmen secretly erected blockades on different roads and stopped all traffic for inspection.

As Auburn was recovering from the economic woes of the Great Depression, there was great trouble in Europe. The German invasion partitioned Poland between Germany and Russia. Soviet forces seized Lithuania, Latvia, and Estonia and invaded Finland. United States allies England and France declared war on Germany.

9. Rationing, Telegrams, and Red Devils: The War Years (1940–1954)

Yesterday, Dec. 7, 1941 a date which will live in infamy—the United States of America was suddenly and deliberately attacked by naval and air forces of the Empire of Japan . . . I ask that the Congress declare that since the unprovoked and dastardly attack by Japan on Sunday, Dec. 7, a state of war has existed between the United States and the Japanese empire.

~Franklin Delano Roosevelt, Pearl Harbor Speech, December 8, 1941

The war years generated profound changes in the United States and in Auburn, both temporary and permanent. The rationing of many consumer products was only a temporary inconvenience to Auburn's households, compared to the soldiers who gave years of their lives or, indeed, made the ultimate sacrifice. The Western Union messenger's walk to the door was a dreaded sight. Western Union telegrams usually told families of the injury or death of their loved ones.

The innocence, relative isolation, and complacency of this heartland town was lost forever as America entered the cold war years, with its bomb shelters and nuclear attack emergency supplies.

Daily life went on even as the focus of industries changed to war production. Diversions included following the Auburn Red Devils basketball team—which went to the Indiana State Basketball Final Four Tournament in 1949—and making summer trips to Circle Park or Cold Springs.

When war erupted in Europe in 1939, Americans debated whether they should get involved. The United States shifted its policy from neutrality to preparedness and began to expand its forces, build defense plants, and give its allies all-out aid.

"Uncle Billy" Stafford, Auburn's last Civil War veteran, died in May 1939, just before Auburn began preparing for the second "war to end all wars." In September 1940, the DeKalb County Free Fall Fair was cancelled due to the mounting war effort. In October 1940, the DeKalb County office registered 2,589 men in compliance with the Selective Service Law.

Recruiting in the county began in the fall of 1940 and, on November 22, 1940, Ellsworth K. Saxer and Robert Thrush of rural Garrett and Ragard Whitely of Ashley were the first volunteers.

On April 15, 1941, 66 men left DeKalb County for the Army. On May 20, 1941, 4,500 soldiers from Camp Custer camped in DeKalb County for the night. On November 18, Warren Lige was appointed DeKalb County director of civilian defense and, on November 26, Earl Fribley was appointed chairman of defense activities in Auburn.

Japan's attack on Pearl Harbor on December 7, 1941 was the act that tipped the scales to full participation in the war. President Franklin D. Roosevelt called December 7 "a date which will live in infamy." On December 11, 1941, war was declared on Japan, Germany, and Italy.

The Declaration of War was received in Auburn by radio. Soon, the entire city was mobilizing. World War II set in motion an incredible amount of bureaucracy. There was a county committee for every facet of the war effort. Most committees were federal in origin, but were administered on a state and county basis.

The first DeKalb County casualty was John Wesley Deetz, whose name was released on May 6, 1942. On May 28, 1942, a memorial service was held for

WORLD WAR II MEMORIAL. The memorial in the rotunda of the DeKalb County Courthouse contains the names of all DeKalb County soldiers killed in World War II and subsequent wars.

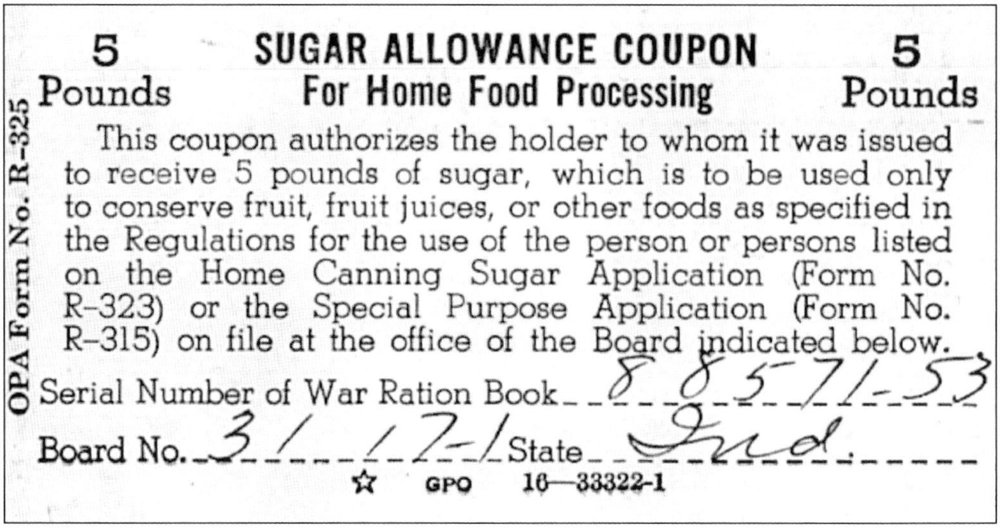

5 **SUGAR ALLOWANCE COUPON** 5
Pounds **For Home Food Processing** Pounds

This coupon authorizes the holder to whom it was issued to receive 5 pounds of sugar, which is to be used only to conserve fruit, fruit juices, or other foods as specified in the Regulations for the use of the person or persons listed on the Home Canning Sugar Application (Form No. R-323) or the Special Purpose Application (Form No. R-315) on file at the office of the Board indicated below.

Serial Number of War Ration Book 885 71-53

Board No. 31 / 17-1 State Ind.

☆ GPO 16—33322-1

OPA Form No. R-325

SUGAR ALLOWANCE COUPON. Home canning of garden-grown foods was encouraged, so coupons for extra sugar were available for such purpose.

Deetz and Richard Williamson. News of casualties and soldiers missing in action became commonplace, but hard to accept.

There was not a citizen of Auburn who was not affected in some way by the war. Most had a family member in service. Women went to work in factories. Volunteers were solicited for every conceivable activity. DeKalb County school children were called upon to collect milkweed pods, the silk from which was used to make life preservers. In December 1943, 1,600 bushels were collected, enough to make 800 life preservers.

Everything was regulated. Most people were frozen in their jobs at pre-war wages. Many worked seven days a week. People made good money, but there were few items to purchase. Virtually everything was in short supply or not available at all. Most put their earnings into war bonds.

Air raid drills and blackouts were practiced in our towns. DeKalb County was prepared for attack. Our defenses were ready.

The local civilian bureaucracy was massive: Selective Service Board—classified all registrants; Governmental Appeal Agent—heard appeals from the Selective Service Board; Examining Physician and Dentists—gave physical examinations to registrants; Bond Sales Committee—promoted sale of war bonds; Re-employment Committee—assisted returning veterans to obtain employment; Procurement and Assignment Service—listed all medical and veterinarian personnel for special classification; American Red Cross, DeKalb County Chapter—recruited volunteers for war effort; Indiana War Fund—coordinated fundraising efforts of charities seeking funds for war effort; Legal Services Committee—gave free legal service to families of soldiers and retiring veterans; Victory Book Collection—solicited books to send to service persons; Salvage Committee—recycled materials, such as iron, aluminum, paper, and kitchen grease; U.S. Department of Agriculture War Board—allocated proper distribution of food supply; Home Demonstration Agents—assisted in food conservation; Farm Credit Association—gave loans for food production; Office of Price Administration—handled rationing coupons and regulated price of certain items; War Finance Committee—encouraged savings through war bonds and stamps; Civil Defense Committee—coordinated civil defense; Air Warning Service—warned of air attacks; Engineering Advisory Committee—primarily assisted in maintaining local roads and bridges; Emergency Water and Sewage Service—gave mutual assistance in the event of sabotage of utilities; Care of Children in Wartime Committee—provided care of children of working mothers; and Civil Air Patrol—assisted military in air patrols. Hundreds of local people were involved in these committees, most of which were organized on a county basis.

The Civil Defense Committee organized the town into "blocks" and staged blackouts, at which times residents were required to extinguish all sources of light to keep the town less visible from the air in the event of a night attack. The committee also staged mock bomb attacks to practice rescue efforts in the event of an actual bombing.

The quick and complete transformation of the nation's industrial base into a war machine was incredible. Industry that survived the Depression was gradually recovering. Suddenly, the nation was at war. Most regular production was stopped and the companies were ordered by the government to manufacture war items consistent with their manufacturing capacity.

For example, Borg-Warner Corporation, which manufactured automotive after-market parts, was ordered to manufacture the small two-cylinder gasoline engines that provided the power for the generators to create interior electric power in B-29 aircraft. The plant was surrounded with an 8-foot chain link fence for security. Employees had to wear photo identification badges for entry into the plant.

The Rieke Corporation made flanges for steel drums. During World War II, Rieke developed the "blitz plug" and flange combination for the 5-gallon "jerry" gasoline container. The Rieke Corporate airplane, a DC-3, was confiscated by the government for war use. Glen Rieke told that his company received a telegram that an agent of the government would arrive on a certain day to take possession of their plane. The agent the government sent was a pilot, who wrote out a receipt "the size of a postcard and flew our plane away. We never saw it again but eventually got fair compensation for it."

Compared to the horrors of actual war, homefront privations were next to nothing. It was considered not only patriotic, but also necessary, for *all* civilians to do their part.

The economy was not nearly so global in those years, but still, many items of everyday life were imported. Coffee, bananas, sugar, rubber, and other items came to the United States by ship. Rubber, particularly, came from areas in the South Pacific that the Japanese were invading. Shipping not only was dangerous, but all available ships were pressed into urgent war duty.

Domestic goods, such as oil and gasoline, clothing, particularly leather for shoes, and almost all foods, were needed for "the war effort."

Nevertheless, civilians had to eat, wear clothes, and get from place to place, so a system of rationing was devised to distribute hard-to-get goods more fairly. Issuing ration books and coupons, especially determining fairness, was a gargantuan job. It is a marvel that it was accomplished by the end of 1942, with the most critical items, such as gasoline, rationed as early as May 1942.

Each county had a "rationing board" made up of citizen volunteers. The head of each household had to come before the board in order to receive books of rationing stamps for each family member. Children, however, did not get coffee stamps. Anyone who thought they needed more of something could appear before the board and state the circumstances, and the board would make a decision. The items most argued over were tires, gasoline, sugar, and shoes.

Ration stamps became almost more important than money. Consumers could not buy most things without them, no matter how much money they had. In a grocery store, for instance, each item was tagged with two amounts: the price and the number of coupons needed. There was also color coding. Meat needed red coupons, whereas canned vegetables needed green, so one could not plan a splurge on steaks by saving up food coupons.

Gasoline was perhaps the sorest point of all. Drivers were rated as "essential" or "non-essential." The stamps issued for gasoline were pasted to the windshield. Class A drivers were deemed non-essential and got the least gasoline—perhaps 5 gallons per week. Class B stamps were for those who drove in their work or to essential war-related jobs. Class C stamps were for especially essential drivers, such as doctors. Tires were allotted along much the same lines.

World War II families found they could augment their allotments by raising Victory Gardens, along with their own backyard chickens. Those who had farmer friends could sometimes get chickens or other meat direct through a "black market" system. Families also traded rationing coupons for items that they wanted. For example, someone who smoked cigarettes, but did not use much sugar, might trade their sugar coupons for cigarette coupons.

Recycling of some things was encouraged. Every tin can was washed, the bottom removed, the can crushed into a flat piece of metal, the two ends inserted into the crushed can, and then saved for pickup for recycling. Grease from fried foods was also saved. The Auburn Rubber Company manufactured "Stick on Soles," a rubber shoe tread or heel that could be glued to the bottom of a worn out pair of shoes. A small tube of glue was supplied along with instructions as to how to accomplish the transplant.

The end of World War II generated a massive celebration on the courthouse square. News reached Auburn shortly after 6:00 p.m. on August 14, 1945. Within minutes, whistles, bells, sirens, and other noisemakers were heard in celebration of the victory.

Most churches were opened for services of thanksgiving. Later, a large crowd gathered on the square. There were many impromptu parades around the square.

The Auburn Civilian Defense Council

has divided the city into 10 Sectors

This Home is in Sector No. 8

Your Senior Warden is John Burtner

Address 1111 S. Main Tel. No. 869-MX

Your Block Warden is Jack Olinger

Address S. Wayne Tel. No. 139

THE AUBURN CIVILIAN DEFENSE COUNCIL. The home at 1111 South Main Street was in Section 8 and Jack Olinger was the block warden. Homeland security was closely guarded during World War II.

During the evening, Jay Van Zile organized an impromptu band that played near the war memorial on the southwest corner of the square. The American Legion and the Moose Lodge presented the colors.

Noise was the order of the evening—firecrackers, shotguns, automobile backfire, and a group from the 40 & 8, an elite World War I unit, shot their salute cannon on the square. There were numerous vehicles in the parades, from horse-drawn wagons to large trucks from the Auburn Foundry. The real celebrations took place later, one by one, as DeKalb County's soldiers came home to their families, sweethearts, and wives.

Sixty-nine DeKalb County servicemen lost their lives in World War II. The Memorial Monument of Deceased War Heroes was erected in the rotunda of the DeKalb County Courthouse and dedicated July 24, 1947. The triangular obelisk is 8 feet high and contains the names of those county men who lost their lives.

Auburn was no more ready for the Korean War than was the rest of the nation. Our people were recovered from World War II; the economy was good, employment was high, and those who had served long and hard were enjoying the fruits of the democracy they had so avidly defended. Few were ready for another major military operation. Many were afraid that another world war would result. But they served willingly when the time came.

The Japanese gained control of Korea in 1895 and made it part of Japan in 1910. When the Allies defeated Japan in World War II, the United States and Russian forces moved into Korea, with Russia north of the 38th parallel and the

United States south of the 38th parallel. In 1947, the United Nations declared that elections were to be held in Korea to choose one government for the entire country. Russia opposed this concept and refused to permit elections. On May 10, 1948, South Korea elected a national assembly and set up the government of the Republic of Korea. On September 9, 1948, the North Korean Communists established the Democratic Peoples Republic of Korea. Both North Korea and South Korea claimed all of the Korean Peninsula.

The war began on June 25, 1950, when North Korea invaded South Korea. The United Nations called the invasion a violation of international peace and demanded that the North Koreans withdraw. The United Nations asked its member nations to give military aid to South Korea. Sixteen member nations sent troops, with the United States supplying over 90 percent. China and Russia aided the North Koreans. The war "ended" on July 27, 1953 when the United Nations and North Korea signed a truce. A permanent peace treaty has not been signed to date and the 38th parallel remains an armed and fortified border.

Over 700 DeKalb County soldiers served during the Korean War, with 14 DeKalb County men losing their lives. Their names were added to the memorial monument located in the courthouse.

Sports were the principle diversion during this era. Most industries had company teams in baseball and softball. These were adult teams comprised of employees of that industry. In some cases, employees were hired on the basis of their athletic skills rather than their production skills.

High school teams were particularly competitive in the age of classless sports; that is, when all the teams in Indiana competed against each other, regardless of size. Auburn was always "the team to beat" in basketball and football. Alumni Gym, adjacent to McIntosh High School in the 700 Block of South Main Street, was opened on December 5, 1924, and was the scene of many "barn burner" basketball games. It seated 2,400 persons, about half of the population of Auburn at the time. It was the home of the Auburn Red Devils, who went to the Indiana High School Athletic Association state finals in 1949. The team lost to Jasper in the afternoon game. One local minister attributed the loss to the name "Red Devil." The team was coached by Keith Showalter and included members Roger Wertenberger, Don Derrow, Bob Bates, Jim Schooley, Ken McInterf, Bud McComb, Theo Webb, Barney Beers, and Don Kelly.

Area coaches used many strategies to defeat the dreaded Red Devils. In 1952, the Butler Windmills' coach used a stall strategy. The score was 7 to 4—with Auburn winning of course. This Red Devil win was preceded by a crushing defeat of the Ashley Aces—92 to 34!

With two major wars concluded, the war hero Dwight David Eisenhower as President, and a bustling economy, Auburn and the nation were ready to enter a new era.

10. ELVIS, THE BARONS, AND THE CANTEEN: MID-CENTURY (1955–1969)

And so, my fellow Americans; ask not what your country can do for you—Ask what you can do for your country.

~Inaugural Address of President John F. Kennedy, Washington, D.C., January 20, 1961

Auburn's Baby Boomers grew up during this era and consider it the golden era of their hometown. Mid-century found Auburn the epitome of a Midwestern county seat, with tree-lined streets, front porches, and good neighbors. Although sobered and somewhat wary due to the loss of the city's major industry and a recent world war, it was a prosperous, happy time in most respects.

Auburn was mostly self contained with nearly everything needed available locally. Grocery stores were convenient, clothing stores complete, and the Auburn City Hardware flatly advertised "We Have It." And they probably did! The Court Theatre and the Smart Theatre showed first-run movies. The Auburn Rubber Company was turning out rubber cars, trucks, cows, and horses by the millions and even added a second plant at Connellsville, Pennsylvania.

The Boomers's parents were concerned by the pelvic gyrations of Elvis Presley and then by the invasion of long-haired "Beetles" from England. The Red Devils still dominated regional sports and were the symbol—the icon—of the perceived superiority of Auburn and its residents.

Dwight Eisenhower had passed through our area in 1918 on the Lincoln Highway as a lieutenant in the U.S. Army caravan demonstrating the value of motorized vehicles and the need for good roads in the interest of national defense. With two recent wars concluded and national defense of great concern, Eisenhower recognized the need for a national highway system that could be used to quickly mobilize defense capabilities in the event of an attack. Interstate 69 was projected through DeKalb County. This highway was to have as profound an effect on Auburn as had the railroads a century before.

There were seeds of change evolving, however. Philo T. Farnsworth's 1927 invention of electronic television was bringing the rest of America, and indeed the world, into our living rooms. Auburn even had an early television station—almost!

The second station in the Fort Wayne market was WIN-T, which had its studio in Waterloo and its transmitter and tower on County Road 29 south of Auburn, a facility later used by WIFF radio.

The origin of DeKalb County's television station was very controversial and led to a congressional investigation. The FCC licensed the station to a consortium of Cleveland and Detroit interests in 1953. The station was ostensibly to serve the Angola area, which was far enough away from Fort Wayne to warrant its own license. The licensee corporation was Tri-State Television, Inc.

In reality, the licensee wanted to serve the Fort Wayne market area, for which no additional television license was then available. The law provided that a television studio could be located within a certain radius from the city to which the license was granted. Waterloo was within the range permitted for Angola. The law further provided that the transmitter could be located within a certain radius from the studio. A point about 2 miles south of Auburn on County Road 29 was within the range permitted from the studio in Waterloo. Thus, by leapfrogging the ranges of distance prescribed by the law, the transmitter was located within about 16 miles of Fort Wayne, close enough to serve that market.

This subterfuge of the law permitted the Angola licensee to parley the Angola license, which was of little value, into one that was very valuable. In 1956, the station was sold to Universal Broadcasting Company of Indianapolis for as much

AUBURN HARDWARE, "WE HAVE IT." Auburn Hardware is the successor to Pioneer Hardware and has been in business at this location since 1850. Merchandise was displayed in second-story windows as well as ground-floor windows.

as $10 million. It is likely that this transaction included several other stations, so the price for WIN-T was likely less. Nevertheless, this transaction resulted in a Congressional investigation of the way television licenses were granted, bought, and sold. As a result, there were changes in the law and more stations were authorized in order to diminish the value of the original stations. WIN-T first telecast on September 29, 1954 from the former bus station building on South Wayne Street in Waterloo.

Even in the 1950s and 1960s there was little reason a family needed to leave Auburn. When the author, with his wife Barbara Clark Smith and young son John Clark Creager Smith, moved to Auburn in July 1965, he purchased the town house of former DeKalb County Auditor Miles Waterman at 506 South Jackson Street. Nearly every need was within walking distance of this home. The Presbyterian Church was across the street; Dr. John Hines was two blocks to the northeast; the McKinney-Harrison elementary school was two blocks west; Auburn High School was two blocks south; Souder Hospital was six blocks north; there were three service stations, the Texaco to the north and the Cities Service and Standard to the east; the Eckhart Public Library was diagonally across the street; and the Auburn Post Office was three blocks north.

The downtown area was three blocks to the north and east. The family could walk nearly everywhere. The author walked to his law office at 110 West Eighth Street, and walked home for lunch and a nap at noon. The downtown was full of stores that supplied nearly every need. Clothing could be purchased at Schaab's Department Store; menswear at Landy's, later Hoham's Menswear; hardware and housewares at Auburn City Hardware, the Gamble Store, and Culbertson's; records and record players at Cooper's Music Store; groceries at Kroger's, Atlantic and Pacific Tea Company (A&P), and Swartz's; meat at Bowermans; jewelry at Carbaugh's, Owen's, and Poore's; Furniture at Gerig's; toys, notions, and miscellaneous at National 5&10 Store and J.J. Newberry Company; drugs and sodas at Romeiser's and Wildermuth's; appliances and televisions at All Appliance; and popcorn on a warm summer evening at Martha's Popcorn Stand on Ninth Street.

The family car was often not used for a week at a time. Trips to Fort Wayne were rare, but usually made twice per year, often at the beginning of school and prior to Christmas.

Downtown restaurants included the City Café, The 113 Restaurant, Reuters Restaurant, the Tee Pee, the Auburn Hotel Restaurant and Lounge, and the Auburn Diner. The City National Bank, Auburn State Bank, Peoples Savings and Loan, and Auburn Federal competed for banking business and were all locally owned.

Automobiles could be purchased and serviced at Rohm Chevrolet and Buick, Auburn Motor Sales (Ford), Dailey Motors (Plymouth, Dodge, and Chrysler) and Bassett Motor Sales (Oldsmobile).

First-run movies could be seen at the elegant Court Theatre with its "Spanish Villa" interior architecture and atmospheric ceiling that simulated the night sky.

Milk and related products were delivered to the door by the Auburn Dairy or the Midwest Dairy.

For those who lived a bit farther from the square, there were neighborhood groceries: the Little Dutch Grocer at 749 North Jackson Street, City Market at 430 South Indiana Avenue, Hoover Grocery at 906 East Fifth Street, Lemish Grocery and Market at 609 North Jackson Street, and Lung's Superette at Division Street and the Old Brick Road. White's Westwood Super Dollar Market was at 801 West Seventh Street and Burger's IGA was at 1424 Wayne Street.

Other Auburn merchants included Fetzer's Bakery at 208 North Main where they should have charged extra for the aroma of fresh baked goods; Vesta Graham Cider Mill at 1902 South Wayne Street where one could get apples pressed into fresh cider in season; Gengnagel and Hoodelmier Coal Companies which would deliver coal, lump, or stoker to your bin; Auburn Hatchery and Feed Mill at 225 East Ninth Street where the sound of "peeping" baby chickens usually greeted customers; Auburn Locker service at 105 South Union Street where those who had no freezer kept their quarters or halves of beef or pork; Auburn Ice Company at 1884 Jacob Street where blocks of ice up to 100 pounds could be purchased along with a whiff of ammonia from the mysterious "rattle-trap" machinery that mysteriously made ice; Nor-Ann Shop at 206 East Seventh Street and Willa Marie Millinery Shoppe at 112 North Main Street where ladies could purchase elaborate hats draped in feathers, vines, fruit, flowers, or perhaps a bird, complete with a veil to partially cover the embarrassment of wearing such a concoction; the Railway Express Agency at 209 East Ninth Street where one could ship packages by rail; Nu-Way Shoe Rebuilders at 111 West Ninth Street where one's shoes could be repaired and shined; Signs by Shafer at 1324 South Main where Lee Shafer would paint a sign and give sage advice while you waited; Shooks at 114 East Seventh Street where you could purchase wallpaper to redecorate your home; and Western Union Telegraph Company at 125 West Eighth Street where you could send a telegram or wire money anywhere in the world.

Auburn residents knew it was time to eat when they heard the whistles of the Auburn Foundry and Ball Brass blow at noon. The fire whistle blew at noon on Wednesday and Saturday and whenever necessary to call volunteer firemen to a fire. They responded with their blue lights flashing. The first few to arrive at the fire barn on East Ninth Street rode on the fire truck driven by the lone paid fireman on duty, while later arrivals raced to the fire behind the truck in their personal cars.

Many residents migrated to Hamilton Lake or to other Steuben and Noble County Lakes on weekends or for the whole summer if the family was fortunate enough to own a lake cottage. A steady stream of cars passed through Auburn on State Road 427 from about 4:00 p.m. until dark every summer Sunday.

The Auburn YMCA was the hangout for teenagers. The Canteen provided hamburgers, cheeseburgers, hot dogs, pop, and ice cream sodas. A dance was held every Saturday night with live bands or disk jockeys. The "Y" also had two bowling lanes and a pool where there were certain hours for boys and certain

LITTLE DUTCH GROCER. The Little Dutch Grocer at the southwest corner of North Jackson and North Streets was a neighborhood grocery.

hours for girls—because bathing suits were not permitted—all swam in the nude! (Presumably, this requirement was for sanitary reasons.)

Those teenagers with cars went to Cold Springs at Hamilton Lake where WOWO disc jockeys Bob Seivers, Bob Chase, Jack Underwood, and Don Chevilet spun records while broadcasting live from coast to coast over the 50,000-watt clear channel station. "Killer" hamburgers and malts were available at the Cold Springs Grill, followed by a stroll to the Cold Spring at lakeside where the dark but moonlit setting provided the perfect venue for a first kiss. More adventurous young men would bring 3.2 percent beer acquired in Ohio. The girls with their hair in pony tails flirted with the flat-topped boys, usually choosing to couple with the one having the coolest convertible. While backseat romances were common, teenage pregnancies were not accepted. The unwed mother had to leave school to have the baby or perhaps even discretely leave town and go to a "home for unwed mothers" where the newborn child would be placed for adoption.

Pokagon Pop made at Angola was the drink of choice along with the Berg's Bottling Company's Seven-Up, bottled at their plant at 428 Michigan Avenue. No home was without an ample supply of Sechler's Pickles and County Line Cheese cut to within an "nth" of the pound requested from a 40-pound wheel, usually located on top of the butcher case.

The Agar Bug Company moved to Auburn from Butler in 1956. Its owner Amos G. Rimmel manufactured artificial fishing flies with cork bodies and cork

THE MIRACLE OF INDIANA. The citizens of DeKalb County built the DeKalb Memorial Hospital with no governmental involvement. It was opened on January 2, 1964.

ice fishing bobbers. Many local teenagers were hired to work in the plant at 711 Hazel Street and women were hired to tie flies at home on a piece rate.

Prior to 1961, Auburn had two hospitals. The Souder Hospital at 205 West Sixth Street was founded in 1915 by Dr. Ulysses Grant Souder and his daughter Dr. Bonnell M. Souder, who was a pioneer in maternity care. During her long career, she delivered thousands of babies, including the author. In 1925, J.A. Sanders M.D. opened Sanders General Hospital at 1007 South Main Street. Gradually, these two private hospitals became inadequate for the growing town. There was also a small hospital at Garrett.

The history of DeKalb Memorial Hospital began in 1955 when the Auburn Lion's Club authorized a group of men to see if there was a need for a new hospital in DeKalb County. In 1956, the Auburn Lions hired Dr. Herman Smith of Chicago to make a professional survey. Out of this came a petition circulated among the people asking the county to set up a fact-finding committee. Judge Harold D. Stump, DeKalb circuit court judge, named an eight-man board that was to report to the county commissioners. In June 1960, these eight men, headed by Glenn Rieke of Auburn, laid the facts before the commissioners.

There was a need for new facilities because some of the 79 beds available in the three DeKalb County hospitals did not meet state health requirements. The report also suggested that a citizen-owned facility be built and maintained by the people of the county.

The people, industries, and organizations, along with W.H. Willennar of Auburn, the largest single contributor to the hospital, dug into their pockets and came out with enough money to build a new hospital. There was also enough money to staff and maintain the hospital for the first year. From that time on, the hospital was self-sustaining.

Known as the "Miracle of Indiana" when it opened on January 2, 1964, DeKalb Memorial Hospital has enjoyed a steady growth. The facilities have been expanded numerous times. The Miracle of Indiana has served Auburn and

DeKalb County well through nearly 40 years of operation. The hospital continues to be operated as a private not-for-profit facility and uses no tax dollars because it is well endowed through the generosity of many DeKalb County families.

Pemco Adhesives was established in 1959 to make industrial adhesives in its plant at 1108 Auburn Drive. But the town was shocked when it was announced in 1960 that the Auburn Rubber Company—lock, stock, and molds—had been sold to the town of Deming, New Mexico. As a means of recruiting new industry, Deming was authorized by its state laws to issue bonds to purchase an industry and move it there. The bonds were purchased by the Teamster's Union Pension Fund. Some employees moved to New Mexico with the company, but over 200 were left unemployed in Auburn.

As with the purchase of the Auburn Automobile plant by Borg-Warner in 1938, the town of Auburn was fortunate that Cooper Industrial Products, Inc. of Ohio purchased the former Auburn Rubber Company plant at 725 West 11th Street in the fall of 1960 to resume the production of rubber products. This industry has proved to be one of Auburn's most solid. The Auburn Rubber Company of Deming, New Mexico continued production for several years, but its product quality decreased. The company eventually filed for bankruptcy.

Soon after the Auburn Automobile Company and allied companies went out of business, their vehicles came to be prized by collectors. The cars were appreciated more after the fact than when they were introduced.

In the early 1950s, advertisements began to appear in *Motor Trend* magazine for Auburns, Cords, and Duesenbergs. Locally, Cal Grosscup had the foresight to acquire an Auburn Speedster, an 812 Cord, and a Model J. Duesenberg, which he often displayed in front of his North Van Buren Street home to the delight of lake travelers returning to Fort Wayne on a Sunday evening. Art Fike of Corunna bought a L-29 Cord Cabriolet off a used car lot in Fort Wayne for $500. Forrest Clouse appreciated the early cars and established a private museum called the "Auto Repository" at his home at the northeast corner of First and Cedar Streets in Auburn.

In 1952, Harry Denhard of New York placed an advertisement in *Motor Trend* seeking people interested in Auburn, Cord, and Duesenberg cars to form a club. This resulted in the formation of the Auburn Cord Duesenberg Club in 1952, just 14 years after the last Auburns, Cords, and Duesenbergs left the factory in 1937.

In 1956, the club held its first "reunion" in Auburn. A few dedicated collectors came to Auburn to show off their cars. Visitors stayed at the Auburn Hotel and displayed their cars on the street.

The Auburn Chamber of Commerce recognized the potential of the Auburn Cord Duesenberg Reunion, as it came to be called, and organized a committee to promote and assist it, headed by Del Mar Johnson. Each year, the chamber appropriated a few hundred dollars to pay for postage and advertising. The event kept improving under Johnson's direction.

The largest construction project ever accomplished in DeKalb County was the building of Interstate 69 in the 1960s. Millions of cubic yards of earth were moved and hundreds of thousands of cubic yards of concrete were poured for the road itself, the bridges, and the overpasses. The federal interstate highway system consists of 42,500 miles of four-lane roads. Its official name is the National System of Interstate and Defense Highways.

The interstate was funded 90 percent by the federal government and 10 percent by the State of Indiana. The route of I-69 through DeKalb County was first announced on January 28, 1958, by Lyle Leas, president of the DeKalb–Steuben–Road Improvement Association. The initial route was to "enter DeKalb County from the south at a point approximately one-half-mile west of state road 427 . . . parallel to the state highway at approximately the same distance until it reaches a point southwest of Auburn where it continues north while 427 curves northeast to an interchange on the Smithfield–Grant Township line one mile west of U.S. 27 at the north edge of Waterloo." It was contemplated that U.S. 6 would be rerouted around the north side of Waterloo to meet the interchange. The route would then go north and leave the county about 2.5 miles east of Ashley.

The road was designated as Interstate FAI 04, but no time schedule was set forth. The announcement of the road did not attract much interest in DeKalb County and only warranted a second-page article in the *Evening Star*. Indiana lagged behind in construction of the super highway due to the constitutional prohibition against state indebtedness. Only current receipts from the gasoline tax could be used for the state's matching 10 percent.

A preview of the coming I-69 was presented by Charles Miser, DeKalb County highway superintendent, at a meeting of the Auburn Lions Club at Marvel's Café in the Dana Plant on January 21, 1963. The first segment to be constructed was from the south county line to U.S. 27 west of Auburn. Miser reported that this was to be one of the most heavily structured segments due to structures over Cedar Creek, over the New York Central, Pennsylvania, and B&O Railroads, diamond interchanges at the St. John's Road and U.S. 27, and overpasses for county roads 68, 60, and the south Auburn-Garrett Road.

As much as 320,000 cubic yards of earth were to be removed to provide grades and cuts, 640,000 yards of fill was to be brought in for overpasses, fills, and other construction needs, and 28,000 yards of peat moss were to be removed from soft spots.

The road itself was laid on a base of gravel. Each lane was a 24-foot mat of 10-inch concrete slanted at least 3 inches to provide drainage. Ninety-thousand tons of aggregate were used and 1,540 feet of piling were used for the Cedar Creek structure.

Once the final route was selected, the office of the Indiana Attorney General filed a series of condemnation cases in the DeKalb Circuit Court to secure the right of way. There were a total of 27 cases, some of which were settled and some of which were tried.

The first segment was opened from Dupont Road in Allen County to County Road 60 in DeKalb County on May 30, 1963. The county was so anxious to have access to the new road that temporary access roads were built at County Road 60 until the St. John's Interchange was completed.

Eventually, the entire route was completed through DeKalb County. The road now extends from I-465 on the north edge of Indianapolis to the Canadian border near Port Huron, Michigan. The numbering system begins at I-465. The south DeKalb County line is at mile post 122 and the north DeKalb County line is at mile post 140. The interchanges are numbered by the mile posts and are numbered 126 (Garrett-Auburn, formerly Auburn-St. John's), 129 (State Road 8), 134 (U.S. 6), and 140 (State Road 4). There were rest parks in DeKalb County at mile post 124. The southbound rest park was closed in 2001. Most of I-69 through DeKalb County was completely rebuilt between 1999 and 2001.

Interstate 69 has had a profound effect on the history and future of DeKalb County. The building of railroads in the 1850s and 1860s were essential to the growth and economic well being of DeKalb County in the last century. As the railroads declined in the 1950s and 1960s, the building of I-69 was equally important to the growth and economic well being of the modern county.

Commercial centers have grown and will continue to grow at the interchanges. The Auburn Interchange has changed the geography and complexion of Auburn in many ways. In recent years, small industries have been attracted to sites near I-69 at Ashley and Waterloo.

The super highway led to the demise of several other major roads in the county. The once busy U.S. 27 is now relegated to a county road carrying only local traffic. Road 427, once the primary north-south road through the county, is now known as County Road 427 and carries only local traffic.

I-69 CONSTRUCTION. The construction of Interstate 69 through DeKalb County was a massive undertaking.

Another profound event in the history of the City of Auburn was school reorganization. From the time when residents were required to build a log school house and then elected the teachers and established the term of school, the prevailing theme of the history of education in Indiana and DeKalb County has been ever increasing centralization and standards.

Centralization occurred naturally in DeKalb County with the closing of township schools and shifting of students to larger town and city school systems in the late 1940s and 1950s. This movement became mandatory with the passage by the Indiana General Assembly of the School Reorganization Act of 1959.

In many cases, the school was the activity center of the community. It was the one place where people frequently met and were bound together by a sense of community. The township trustees would lose much of their authority with school reorganization. The athletic teams that had been friendly rivals for years would be merged. There would be no more Butler Windmills, Waterloo Wildcats, or Auburn Red Devils. Some business persons would be hurt when schools were changed or relocated. There were many interests to be considered and weighed. This was done very judiciously and fairly by the Reorganization Committee after many public meetings. The Reorganization Plan provided for a total of five school districts within DeKalb County as follows:

HIGH SCHOOL. This school building was used until the McIntosh Building was constructed in 1918. The building was Romanesque and made of brick and Indiana limestone.

Garrett-Keyser-Butler Community School District.
Composed of the city of Garrett and Keyser and Butler Townships. This district had already been formed prior to reorganization pursuant to an earlier consolidation law.

DeKalb County South Central Community School District.
Composed of the City of Auburn, and Jackson and Union Townships.

DeKalb County Eastern Community School District.
Composed of the City of Butler and Troy, Stafford, Newville, Spencer, Concord, and Wilmington Townships. This district also included the towns of St. Joe and Spencerville.

DeKalb County Northwest United School District.
Composed of the Town of Waterloo, the town of Ashley including the part of Ashley located in Steuben County, and Grant, Smithfield, Richland, and Fairfield Townships.

Hamilton Community School District.
Composed of the Town of Hamilton and Franklin Township in DeKalb County and Osage and Richland Townships in Steuben County.

This plan was submitted to the voters of DeKalb County at the Primary Election held May 8, 1962 and was approved. The first members of the school boards for the respective districts were then appointed by Judge Harold D. Stump. The respective boards began the awesome task of implementing the Reorganization Plan. This was painful to the communities as the plans became a reality. As the Northwest and South Central Boards began examining specific plans and costs, it became apparent that economic and other advantages would result from a merger of these two districts.

The Northwest and South Central Boards met in joint sessions on January 10, 1964 to consider a proposed merger. The merger resolution carried, so the question was put on the ballot for the Primary Election to be held May 5, 1964. Only the voters of the Northwest District voted because their district was merging with the South Central District, with the latter being the surviving district. The voters passed the referendum with 1,057 in favor and 705 against. The two boards then met again in joint session on May 7, 1964 and formally merged into the DeKalb County Central United School District effective July 1, 1964. All trustees of both boards voted in favor of the merger at this meeting. The merger was quickly approved by the State Commission for the Reorganization of School Corporations on May 25, 1964.

The DeKalb Central United School District became effective July 1, 1964. Granville L. Deaton was superintendent from July 1, 1964 to June 30, 1965. Dr. James B. Watson served as superintendent from July 1, 1965 until his retirement. He was succeeded by Keith Perry. To the satisfaction of certain ministers, Auburn's beloved Red Devils were no more, replaced by the non-offensive "Barons," named after the county's namesake Baron DeKalb. New schools were being built to accommodate modified demographics.

Auburn had its own radio station beginning April 10, 1967 when WIFF radio went on the air. The station was started by Wayne Paradise, who was originally from Calumet. He was employed by Mobile Oil Company in Highland, but was a part-time disk jockey on an all religious station. He aspired to own his own station and began looking for an available FM channel that could be purchased inexpensively. He found one assigned to DeKalb County and acquired it in 1964.

He purchased the former transmitter building and tower of WIN-T Channel 15, Waterloo, and began to put together an FM station. He emphasized local news and on-the-spot broadcasts from advertisers' places of business. Soon, an AM frequency became available when WAWK left the 1570 frequency for a new one. WIFF-AM first went on the air in September 1968.

The "middle of the road" music format had become very competitive, so Paradise tried something very different and perhaps risky at the time. WIFF-AM went to an all country music format. The move proved successful and was maintained for many years until a major Fort Wayne station, WQHK-AM, went country. WIFF-FM then became a "beautiful music" station with gospel programming at night.

The *Trading Post* was a popular program for years. Listeners called in items for sale. Local news was strong and popular. The station was sold to WGL-Radio Fort Wayne and the former WIFF facilities are now used to transmit the WGL signal to the Auburn area. Commercial endeavors were changing during this era and locally owned unique establishments were giving way to nationally known chains.

COURT THEATRE. *The Court Theatre marquee was well lit to attract patrons..*

11. Exits and Superstores:
Up to Now (1970–2002)

Auburn—Next Exit.

~I-69 sign

Remove not the ancient landmark, Which thy fathers have set.

~Proverbs 22:28

Old times were good for those who lived in them; but for us, today is better.

~W.H. McIntosh, writing in 1892 about the Auburn of 1862

Auburn has become homogenized! Our distinctive, sometimes unique, stores and restaurants are mostly gone, replaced by fast-food restaurants and chain stores exactly identical to the stores of that multi-million-dollar corporate conglomerate operated in Auburn, New York; Auburn, Nebraska; and Auburn, California.

The aisles of Wal-Mart have become our public square, the best place to randomly see our friends and neighbors. The cool breeze of the front porch has been replaced by the monotonous hum of an air conditioner. We drive nearly everywhere. We do not even have to get out of our cars to do our banking, pick up prescriptions, or get our sack of excess calories at a fast-food restaurant.

Yet, we are the *Classic City*. We have preserved and memorialized our heritage, our character, our sense of ingenuity, and design in our museums. Many of the fruits of the labor of our ancestors have become collectible—the Auburn, Cord, and Duesenberg automobiles; Auburn Rubber Toys; Auburn Postcards; Auburn Model Trains; and even Agar Bugs.

We are proud of our town. We still cheer for the Barons, but lament the class tournament system, designed to place all in a "proper competitive atmosphere," while denying the opportunity to be the legendary Milan Giant Killer!

In 1965, when Interstate 69 opened, the only businesses west of town on State Road 8 were the Dairy Queen (not opened until 1967) and McCollough Service, a Massey Ferguson tractor dealership. Ira Williams's idyllic "City View Farm" with its tree-lined lane and handsome dairy barn was on the south side of State Road 8.

There was no Grandstaff Drive. Fifteenth Street ended at Hazel Street and North Street ended at Indiana Avenue. We are now Exit 129 on I-69. Travelers can bypass us easily, unless drawn off the Interstate by the pangs of hunger, nature's call, or the desire to see classic cars, trucks, trains, or tanks.

To some, our "old town" has become the "Deserted Village" of Goldsmith's poem. Our square, the sacrosanct heart of our town, is still viable. However, it is without several buildings, notably the 1917 jail, the Auburn Diner, and the Odd Fellows Building, which has been replaced by a park, the not-so-interesting solution to toothless gaps around a square.

Our City National Bank is now Wells Fargo Bank, headquartered in San Francisco, and our Auburn State Bank is now National City Bank, headquartered in Houston. We still have Peoples Federal Savings Bank and some new banks: Auburn Banking Center of the Hicksville Bank, Knisely National Bank, and Lake City Bank. The Northway Drive In Restaurant on North Main Street has survived based on its menu of baked steak, beef and noodles, and other non-fast foods served faster than from the end of a line at McDonald's. The Brown House at Cedar and Ensley Streets was the original drive-through restaurant and has survived on the basis of its coney-dogs and soft-serve ice cream cones with a "cherry" on top.

Auburn's industry has evolved with state-of-the-art production facilities that utilize the efficient work ethic of our sons and daughters. The Auburn Foundry, family owned by the Fink family since 1911, operates two plants in Auburn turning out gray iron castings, mainly for the automotive industry. Auburn Foundry, Inc. reported sales of $150 million in 2001 and ranked 71st among all corporations headquartered in Indiana.

Foley Pattern, Inc. has been locally owned by the Foley family since 1930 and is now in its third generation. It produces aluminum castings. Dana Corporation has been acquired by Eaton Corporation and Ball Brass and Aluminum Foundry has been acquired by Evans Industries, Inc.

New industries recruited by the Auburn Chamber of Commerce with the assistance of city government and tax incentives include Foamex, Reynolds Aluminum, Artistic Carton Company, and R.J. Tower. Cooper Industrial Products, now Cooper Standard Automotive, continues to produce rubber parts and Messenger Corporation still prints items for the funeral industry.

Steel Dynamics, Inc., while not located in Auburn, has had a profound effect on the industrial base of the county and in fact, the region. Led by corporate CEO Keith Busse, a DeKalb County native, over 300 acres of land were acquired east of Auburn between State Road 8 and U.S. 6. The company operates a "steel mini-mill" which produces coils of sheet steel, the basic raw material for many industries. The DeKalb County location was chosen because of the convergence of three railroads—CSX, Norfolk and Southern, and Conrail. Because most of the raw material is shipped in by rail and much of the finished products are shipped out by rail, the availability of competitive shipping rates was a must, as was the relatively cheap rates and excellent availability of electric power from

TIME TO SAVE. The clock at 134 West Seventh Street marked the location of Auburn Federal Savings and Loan Association, which merged with Peoples Federal Savings and Loan.

American Electric Power. The proximity to I-69, the building of a new road between U.S. 6 and State Road 8, and substantial tax incentives were also factors. Several supporting and collateral industries have built facilities near the SDI plant: Paragon Steel, Heidtman Steel, New Millennium Steel, New Process Steel, Air Products Corporation, and Feralloy North American Steel.

In 1969, while the author was president of the Auburn Chamber of Commerce, the chamber decided to expand the Auburn Cord Duesenberg Festival. The organization ordered a quantity of souvenirs to sell to the crowds drawn to Auburn to see the cars on the square. The same year, the Jay Cees put on a "bean dinner" on the square. This was the beginning of generating income to offset costs of the event.

In 1972, the idea was conceived of having an antique and classic car auction in conjunction with what had been renamed the Auburn Cord Duesenberg Festival. A meeting was held in early August at the Greenhurst Country Club involving Del Mar Johnson, the author, and Jack Randinelli for the festival, and Russell Kruse, Dean Kruse, and Leo Gephart of Ohio, a classic car dealer. Plans were then formulated for the first auction. A nucleus of cars was supplied by Leo Gephart and others were consigned. The auction was held east of the Dairy Queen on West Seventh Street in the area now occupied by Westedge Mall.

The first auction was a modest success and over $3,000 was raised for the festival. The Kruses and Gephart then formed Kruse Classic Auction Company and held several auctions around the country.

The second auction was held in 1973 at DeKalb High School and was very successful. By this time, the Auburn Chamber of Commerce was holding auction

DUESENBERG. *The first Duesenberg donated to the Auburn Cord Duesenberg Museum was a Model J Boat-tail. From left to right are the donor Don Carr; John Martin Smith, the president of the museum; and Skip Marketti, the executive director of the museum.*

proceeds in excess of $25,000. A faction wanted to use these funds for chamber purposes. This was resisted by festival interests.

In the meantime, the author advocated the establishment of a museum for the cars built in Auburn. It was then decided that the funds held by the chamber for the festival should be designated for museum purposes. As a result of compromise, the Auburn Cord Duesenberg Festival Committee was severed from the chamber.

Two separate not-for-profit corporations were formed—Auburn Cord Duesenberg Festival, Inc. and Auburn Automotive Heritage, Inc. The festival corporation has remained the sponsor of the annual Labor Day event.

The funds held by the chamber were paid over to the Heritage corporation for museum purposes. There was then considerable discussion as to where and how a museum should be established. One group wanted to build a pole building near I-69 to display about 20 cars. The other group, headed by the author, wanted to acquire the former Auburn Automobile Company Administration Building at 1600 South Wayne Street. The latter group prevailed and the Auburn Cord Duesenberg Museum was opened on July 6, 1974, with only the showroom restored. It is considered one of the premier automobile museums in the country and annually attracts over 80,000 visitors to Auburn.

The slogans "The Classic City" and "Home of the Classics" evolved from Auburn Cord Duesenberg Festival promotion.

The Warbirds Museum was formed in 1992 by a group headed by Niles Walton and, in 1988, the author formed the National Automotive and Truck Museum of the United States, Inc. (NATMUS), with the help of Dean Kruse and Del Mar Johnson, to purchase the remaining buildings of the Auburn Automobile Company. The NATMUS museum was opened July 4, 1994, the centennial of the first practical car driven by Elwood Haynes on the Pumpkin Vine Pike near Kokomo.

In 2002, Dean V. Kruse funded the Dean V. Kruse Foundation to build the World War II Victory Museum to house a large collection of World War II vehicles and artifacts purchased in Europe. The foundation will also operate a classic car museum to house Kruse's personal collection.

At the end of the twentieth century the Auburn *Evening Star* published three special sections entitled "Cruising Through the Century" on November 4, December 2, and December 30, 1999—wherein Auburn citizens who played an important role in the history of Auburn during the twentieth century were noted. Those recognized were Charles Eckhart for his role in the Auburn Automobile Company and his gifts of the Eckhart Public Library, the YMCA, and Eckhart Park; W.H. McIntyre for his pioneer efforts in the automobile and truck industries and in the electrification of area cities and towns; E.L. Cord for his resurrection of the Auburn Automobile Company and his innovations in the automotive industry; Allen Graber for his leadership in recruiting industry to Auburn and providing affordable housing; Dean V. Kruse for his vision in creating a world-class antique automobile auction company and his generosity to the Auburn Cord Duesenberg and NATMUS museums; and B.O. Fink for his seminal efforts in establishing and maintaining the Auburn Foundry, Inc. as a leading industry.

Also recognized were the author for his leadership in establishing and nurturing the Auburn Cord Duesenberg Museum and NATMUS and his role as DeKalb County historian and author of many historical articles and books; Dr. Bonnell Souder for her pioneering efforts as a female physician; Guy "Big Wild Bill" Fitzsimmons for his role in early aviation; and Glenn Rieke for his leadership of the Rieke Corporation and in establishing DeKalb Memorial Hospital.

Many names should be added to this list: John P. Widney and William H. McIntosh for their recording of the early history of DeKalb County; John Zimmerman for his role in the Zimmerman Automobile Company and his tireless efforts in municipal improvements in the first decade of the twentieth century; the Potter family—Silas, Lodie, Forrest, Janet, and Glen—who served on the town council and city council, and as mayor and clerk-treasurer of Auburn from 1898 until 1960, a period of 62 years; Alan Leamy and Gordon M. Beuhrig for their innovative designs of Auburns, Cords, and Duesenbergs; Herbert Snow and Cornelius Van Ranst for their innovative engineering of Auburn Cord Duesenberg Automobiles; Del Mar Johnson for his vision in establishing and nurturing the Auburn Cord Duesenberg Reunion, now Festival; John and Mike

Haggerty, Hugh and James Carper; and Robert and Roger Wertenberger and Maurice Winkler, CEOs respectively of the Auburn State Bank, City National Bank, and Peoples Federal Savings and Loan, for their leadership in the banking industry; William H. Willennar for his endowment that has provided many amenities to Auburn, particularly the Willennar Genealogy and History Center of the Eckhart Public Library; Walter and Harold Stump and Paul R. Cherry, judges of the DeKalb Circuit Court, and Charles L. Quinn and Kevin P. Wallace, judges of the DeKalb Superior Court, who have provided honest, evenhanded justice to the county; Mearl and Irene Bisel for their philanthropy to the community; H.L. McKinney, James R. Watson, and Keith Perry for their leadership of our school systems; and George Witwer, Jim Kroemer, Terry Householder, and Dave Kurtz, who have published and edited the *Evening Star*, one of the best small town daily newspapers in Indiana.

Those mayors, city council persons, and members of the boards and commissions should also be recognized, along with the hundreds of volunteers who have made our town a better place.

The Fort Wayne metropolitan area is creeping toward Auburn from the south. What will the next century bring? A future historian must record, analyze, and unravel it for future generations.

OLD ELM. Auburn's Old Elm was located between South Jackson and Main Streets in the middle of West Thirteenth Street. It was the subject of many photographs and postcards. The Old Elm died in the 1930s, but a descendant survives in the block surrounded by South Main and Jackson Streets and West Thirteenth and Fourteenth Streets.

DIGGING DEEPER:
BIBLIOGRAPHY AND SOURCES

Intelligent men profit by history. The intelligent young man reads back, then looks forward.
~E.L. Cord

The format of this book did not permit footnotes, but there are many statements and clues as to sources. Sources are given for direct quotes. Where dates of events are provided, one can usually go to the newspaper microfiche for that date or shortly thereafter and locate contemporary sources. There are six prior general histories of DeKalb County plus a little-known general index.

The first publication was *Pioneer Sketches; Containing Facts and Incidents of the Early History of Dekalb County*, which was written by S.W. Widney and published by W.T. and J.M. Kinsey, Auburn, in 1859. The original book contained 53 pages. It contains "sketches" of the history of the various towns and townships written by the pioneers of these areas and supplemented by Reverend Widney. The book contains sketches written by Wesley Park and John Houlton. DeKalb County is indeed fortunate to have this early history of the county recorded and published less than 25 years after the county was settled. The book was reprinted in paperback with an index in 1968 by the DeKalb County Historical Society. The reprint is readily available.

In 1880, J.H. Beers and Company of Chicago published *Atlas of DeKalb County, Indiana to which are added Various General Maps, History, Statistics, Illustrations, Etc. Etc.* No author is given in the book. It was probably prepared by the staff of the publishers from information gathered from the public while they were soliciting advance sales for the books. It contains a credible history of the county and several family histories. Its greatest use, however, is for the maps of the towns and townships and the lithograph views of farms and houses throughout the county. The *Atlas* was reprinted in 1974 by The Bookmark, Knightstown, Indiana, but is now out of print. The reprint edition contains a new index and new church and cemetery information not found in the original edition.

The first comprehensive history of DeKalb County was published in 1885, probably in observation of the 50th anniversary of the authorization of the county in 1835 by the Indiana General Assembly. The large leather-covered book is titled *1885 History of DeKalb County, Indiana, Together with Sketches of its Cities, Villages and Towns, Education, Religious, Civil, Military, and Political History, Portraits of Prominent Persons, and Biographies of Representative Citizens*. It was published by Inter-State Publishing Company of Chicago. The book is generally accurate and is useful to the student of DeKalb County History. It contains numerous biographical sketches of DeKalb County residents. The book was sold on a subscription basis for $12. There was also a charge to have one's family history and likeness printed, so only those who were able to afford it had their history or picture printed. As with the 1880 *Atlas*, no author is stated, but the prospectus proclaims that "Our historians are now at work in the county, and would deem it a favor to meet any citizens, especially those who may have anything of historical interest to contribute." It is likely that the "historians" also solicited orders for the book. The 1885 *History* was reprinted in 1978 by The Bookmark, Knightstown, Indiana, with a new index. The reprint is now out of print.

Next is the *History of DeKalb County, Indiana, with Biographical Sketches of Representative Citizens and Geneological* [sic] *Records of Old Families*, published in 1914 by B.F. Bowen and Company, Inc., Indianapolis. It too was published on a subscription basis and does not list an individual author. The book contains 1,004 pages, including many biographical sketches for which the subjects paid an additional fee. The book contains some photographs and etchings. It too is useful, but has only a cursory index. The 1914 *History* has not been reprinted.

In 1920, The Lewis Publishing Company of Chicago and New York published the two-volume *History of Northeast Indiana-LaGrange, Steuben, Noble and DeKalb County*. It is indicated that William H. McIntosh was the editor for DeKalb County. A total of 143 pages is devoted to DeKalb County in volume one. There are also biographical sketches of DeKalb County citizens in volume two and there is an index. This book has not been reprinted.

A little-known adjunct to these prior general histories of DeKalb County is the *DeKalb County, Indiana, Index of Names of Persons and of Firms* completed by the Works Progress Administration (WPA) of Indiana as Work Project 20205 in 1938 under the sponsorship of the Indiana State Library. The index includes all five of the previously listed general histories of DeKalb County. Page numbers are coded to distinguish the book to which they refer. This index has never been published, but photographically reproduced copies of the typescript are available at most DeKalb County libraries, the Fort Wayne–Allen County Public Library, and the Indiana State Library. The *WPA Index* and the new indexes in the reprinted volumes are very useful; however, they contain only names and not concepts. For example, the name "New York Central," would appear, but the general concept of "railroads" would not. There is considerable local historical data hidden in the biographical sketches that does not appear in the index or table of contents.

The sixth and most comprehensive history of DeKalb County is by the author of this volume. *DeKalb County 1837-1987* was published in observance of the Sesquicentennial of DeKalb County in 1990. The work is in two volumes containing 1,511 pages, with a comprehensive index. A companion volume (volume three) contains family histories and was edited by Troas M. Wise. It also contains a comprehensive index of names. The two-volume set is still available for purchase.

These six general histories, plus the present volume, are recommended to the researcher of DeKalb County history as a beginning point for general historical research.

Public records are a rich source of DeKalb County history, but are often difficult to use. While the 1913 courthouse fire destroyed some records, many records remain. Only the records of the clerk of DeKalb Circuit Court were nearly all destroyed. Records since 1913 have been microfilmed and the originals have been deposited with the DeKalb County Historical Society.

The records in the office of the DeKalb County recorder are particularly useful. The Miscellaneous Record was used to record many documents prior to 1900. The author has culled the Miscellaneous Record for much of the source material in this volume. Where dates are given as "hidden footnotes," the person wanting to do additional research can probably locate the original source material. Land records in the recorder's office are also often useful.

Court records since 1913 can be searched for dates of death, divorce, litigation, and other facts. There are records in both the circuit court and superior court.

FOUR-BOWL DRINKING FOUNTAIN. Two well-dressed ladies make use of the fountain on the west side of the square.

WATCHMAN'S SHANTY. Before the advent of automatic signals, railroads stationed watchmen to stop traffic for trains. This shanty was located on the Vandalia Railroad crossing on Wayne Street.

Commissioners records go back to 1837 and contain much information as to county government, roads, jails, elections, and other matters under the jurisdiction of the board of commissioners.

The City of Auburn Minutes are available in the office of the clerk-treasurer. Public records are generally difficult to use unless one has a date. Most are chronological, but not indexed. There is often so much detail that only the most persistent researcher can find them useful.

Newspapers are probably the most fertile source for the researcher of Auburn history, but, like public records, are tedious and difficult to use without background information and dates. All known newspaper archives of DeKalb County have been micro-filmed by the Indiana State Library and are available through interlibrary loan. The Eckhart Public Library, Auburn, has a complete set and continues to microfilm DeKalb County newspapers.

There are many news articles to be found giving the "history" of various topics. Most are quite accurate, although facts should be corroborated with other sources. If one has the approximate date of death of a person who lived in Auburn, it is likely that a detailed obituary can be found. Likewise, if one has the date of an event, it will probably have been reported locally, although early Auburn newspapers are disappointing in the amount of local news carried, as compared with the coverage of national news.

Several special editions of newspapers in Auburn have carried historical material. Examples include the *DeKalb County Herald* of September 6, 1907 and the *Evening Star* "Cruising Through the Century" series of November and December 1999.

An often overlooked source of local history is the information contained in city directories and telephone directories. These sources contain names, addresses, and sometimes the occupations of residents. Often, the names and occupations of spouses are listed. Firm names and locations are also given with the names of principal owners. Directories carried advertisements, which are useful in many cases.

The earliest directory encountered is *Kramer's General Business Directory of Northern Indiana* published in 1884 at Lafayette, Indiana. It contains business directories for Auburn and a full-page advertisement for the Auburn Church Furniture Company, manufacturers of pews, pulpits, and pew ends.

The first DeKalb County Directory was *Moore's Standard Directory of Auburn, Garrett, Butler, and Waterloo*, published in 1908 and 1909 by the S.H. Moore Company of New York City. It contains a wealth of information, including several advertisements for early auto and buggy companies.

From that time on, there were directories published every few years for Auburn.

Telephone directories have just the name, address, and telephone number, but are useful in locating places of residence or business locations. Here also the advertisements can be invaluable.

The first comprehensive map of DeKalb County was published in 1863 by E.B. Gerbe and C.A.O. McClellan. It is a large wall map with farms and their owners shown in the township maps. Shown also are town and village maps and a business directory. Vignettes around the edge picture homes and businesses in Auburn. Several copies of the map are extant, including those hanging in the courthouse and in the waiting room of the law office of John Martin Smith and Thompson Smith, P.C. A separate map of Auburn was published in 1874 by J.S. Bird and Company, Jackson, Michigan. The only known copy is at the office of John Martin Smith and Thompson Smith, P.C.

There are several hundred postcards depicting Auburn. They are a great source of information and illustrations for the period from about 1900 to 1930. Many are used in this volume. Selected DeKalb County postcards have been published in the author's *DeKalb County in Vintage Postcards*, published by Arcadia Publishing in 2001 as a part of its *Postcard History Series.*

The Tri Kappa Collection at the Auburn-Cord-Duesenberg Museum contains thousands of photographs of the automobiles made in Auburn. There is also a collection of mid-1970s photographs at the Eckhart Public Library showing various locations throughout Auburn.

The Internet has become a fertile source of local historical material. Dedicated genealogists, such as Arlene Goodman and Lucy Funk, have transcribed voluminous material, primarily from newspaper sources. The series of articles by William H. McIntosh that appeared in the *Auburn Courier* from October 2, 1890, to January 25, 1894 is on the Internet and has been extensively used as source material in this volume. Citations are not provided here, but generally can be searched under the Eckhart Public Library site.

The William H. Willennar Genealogy and History Center at 700 South Jackson Street, Auburn, operates as an adjunct of the Eckhart Public Library and was dedicated June 22, 2002. It is a major depository for local and regional genealogical and historical material. The center is a gift of the William H. Willennar Foundation. Willennar was president or chairman of the board of the Auburn State Bank from 1930 to 1961. The trustees of the William H. Willennar Foundation are Michael Hagerty, also a former president of the Auburn State Bank; Marcia Close Korwin, granddaughter of Willennar; and Suzanne Zeisloft.

Persons in possession of local historical and genealogical materials should consider donating them to the William H. Willennar Genealogy and History Center so that they can be preserved for future generations.

Local history and genealogy is fun and rewarding. May future historians continue the tradition of recording and disseminating local history!

AUBURN BIG SIX. A 1913 Auburn Big Six is shown in the snow in front of the Eckhart Public Library on South Jackson Street. All cars were test driven before the body was installed.

INDEX